The Metropolitan Transportation Authority - New York City Transit, a state public benefit corporation, administers the New York City Transit Train Operator and Conductor exams. Its parent agency and affiliated subsidiaries were not involved in the production of, and does not endorse, this product.

Front cover photo credit: Goran Bogicevic © 123RF.com

ISBN-10:1546912460
ISBN-13: 978-1546912460

TABLE OF CONTENTS

DISCLAIMER

Neither the author nor publisher claims any responsibility over the outcome of students who use these materials. The views and opinions expressed in this book do not necessarily reflect the official policy, position or perspective of the author, publisher and the MTA. The information contained in this book is used only to facilitate the development of questions, answer choices and explanations to the test questions for the purposes of preparing for the objective civil service exams for Train Operator and Conductor.

Every effort is made in this book to account for the content of the most recently administered 2016 and 2017 conductor and train operator tests. Any changes to the tests after the publication of this book may occur.

1 WHY BUY THIS BOOK?

The book's purpose is to prepare you for the Train Operator or Conductor exam. The objectives of the book are to:

- Earn a high score on the Train Operator or Conductor test by practicing questions that closely reflect the content, style and difficulty level of the real tests and

- Complete the hiring process for Train Operator or Conductor

The book does not prepare you to complete the prescribed New York City Transit (**NYCT**) training course; known colloquially as School Car.

The book offers the following benefits:

- Understanding the New York City civil service process;

- Understanding the requirements to qualify and to take a train operator or conductor exam (open competitive and promotional);

- Knowing the job responsibilities of a train operator and conductor;

- Navigating the hiring and appointment process for train operator or conductor;

- Learning test taking strategies for the train operator or conductor exam;

- Experiencing the train operator or conductor test that closely reflects the real exam taken under simulated testing conditions;

- Reviewing detailed explanations for both the correct and incorrect answers (where relevant) with specific test taking strategies designed for each type of question and

- Thinking like the test writers for the NYCT train operator and conductor exams

2 INTRODUCTION

As I stood amongst the thousands of applicants sitting for the Train Operator exam in 2017, I heard many individuals express similar frustrations of poor quality test preparation books. I have heard similar frustrations in the past when I took the conductor and train operator exams during the 2000s. A commercial test prep book contained obsolete questions with no explanations to the answers. The outdated questions were from past promotional exams for Motorman (now known as Train Operator) and Conductor that were administered in the 1970s.

The lack of quality test preparation materials for the train operator and conductor exams motivated me to prepare a test preparation book that closely reflects the content and difficulty level of previous actual train operator and conductor exams. Each time an exam is given, the author sits through an exam and analyzes the subtle changes in the design and content of the test questions. I am confident that this book will give you an advantage over other test takers vying for this civil service job opportunity.

Although this book is specifically for the train operator and conductor positions with NYCT, it can be used for other civil service exams that test reading comprehension and mathematics. The book familiarizes individuals with the civil service process to obtain a job with the City of New York.

A HISTORY LESSON

Since the 1980s, the job title has been changed from motorman to train operator to reflect females entering into the subway operative position. The train operator title has traditionally been offered as a promotion for current NYCT employees (ie. Bus operator, conductor, station agent, property protection agent, track worker and cleaner). However, NYCT opined in the late 1990s that the agency could attract better quality train operators by hiring non-Transit employees, known colloquially as "off the streets."

NYCT had to prove to Civil Service that the agency was unable to promote from within its own ranks. In January 1998, one thousand eight hundred (1,800) NYCT employees took the promotional train operator test and only thirty-two (32) passed[1]. The unintended consequences of creating a difficult train operator test resulted in a shortage of employees eligible for promotion to train operator. In July 1998, another promotional train operator test was administered to 2,167 Transit employees and eight hundred (800) passed[2]. Armed with these test results, Transit stated its case that the agency had an inadequate pool of qualified candidates for train operator from its ranks. The

---

[1] Farrell, B. (1999). Train Operator's Exam Opening To Public. *New York Daily News.*
[2] Farrell, B. (1999). Train Operator's Exam Opening To Public. *New York Daily News.*

New York City Council held a hearing regarding opening the position to the public. There was a real concern of putting an individual completely unfamiliar with Transit at the controls of a four hundred ton train.

In 1999, NYCT allowed the public to apply for the train operator exam for the first time; known as an open competitive exam. Open competitive exams are offered to the public who do not work in civil service and meet the posted qualifications for a particular job title. The first open competitive exam was administered in January 2000 and the test attracted over twenty-four thousand (24,000) applicants. Both the public and Transit employees filed for the exam. Since the 2000 train operator exam, the exams have been offered separately as **open competitive** and **promotional**. These terms will be explained in the next section.

QUALIFICATIONS TO TAKE THE TRAIN OPERATOR EXAM

OPEN COMPETITIVE TRAIN OPERATOR EXAM

This exam is open to non-civil service individuals who meet the below requirements and to NYCT employees ineligible for promotion to train operator.

Previously, the requirements were a high school diploma or its educational equivalent (eg. GED) and five years of full time satisfactory work experience or a college degree and one year of full time satisfactory work experience. Beginning with the open competitive train operator exam application in December 2016, NYCT changed the requirements below to be eligible for the test.

a.   A four year high school diploma or its educational equivalent;
b.   A Motor Vehicle Driver License **valid** in the State of New York and
c.   One year of full time satisfactory work experience that has been **continuous with one employer**.

All of the above requirements **must** be met by the end of an application deadline for the train operator exam.

PROMOTION TO TRAIN OPERATOR EXAM

a. Eligible NYCT employees who are permanent (ie. completed one year probation) in their title by the time of appointment for train operator. The qualified titles are NYCT Conductor, NYCT Bus Operator or Tower Operator.

b. Or eligible employees who have completed a **Transit Certificate Program (TCP)** for Train Operator with the Transport Workers Union Local 100 to qualify for the promotional exam.

The TCP for Train Operator consist of three classes:

- Worker, Health and Safety (3 college credits)
- An Overview of Transit (3 college credits)
- Job Duties of a Train Operator

Employees who complete all three classes will be eligible to sit for the promotional exam for Train Operator. They can use their six college credits towards a degree subjected to acceptance by a college or university.

Special Notes to MTA Employees:

1. Employees who meet either qualification above must have three (3) years of full-time work experience including at least one (1) year with NYCT.

2. Employees who are still on probation in an eligible title listed above can take the promotional Train Operator. They need to have completed their one year probation by the time they are considered for appointment to train operator.

3. Your exam score will determine 85% of your final score. The remaining 15% is based on your seniority. Your seniority score is calculated as 70 plus ½ (or .5) point for each three (3) months of completed, permanent (non-provisional) and continuous employment with a job title under the Department of Citywide Administrative Services (eg. Department of Finance, Department of Design and Construction). If you have had employment gaps of City employment service of more than one year, no credit is given. Up to a maximum of 15 years is credited for your City service.

Summary:

70+ (.5 point for every 3 months of qualifying City service) =Seniority score

Your final score is calculated based on the following:

(Your multiple choice test score x .85) +(Your seniority score x .15) =Final total score

4. MTA Bus and MABSTOA bus operators and Staten Island Railway Transit Operating Authority (SIRTOA) Conductors are not eligible to take the promotional train operator exam. SIRTOA Conductors are eligible to apply for SIRTOA Locomotive Engineer positions when vacancies occur.

QUALIFICATIONS TO TAKE THE CONDUCTOR EXAM

OPEN COMPETITIVE CONDUCTOR EXAM

1. A four year high school diploma or its educational equivalent

PROMOTION TO CONDUCTOR EXAM

1. Permanent (ie. completed one year probation) employee or on a Preferred List for the title of Railroad Track Cleaner, Cleaner (TA), Station Agent, Transit Property Protection Agent or Collecting Agent; or

2. Employed as a Labor Class Transit Cleaner or Transit Track Cleaner

Special Notes for NYCT Employees:

1. Employees who are still on probation in an eligible title listed above can take the Promotional Conductor exam. They need to have completed their one year probation by the time they are considered for appointment to Conductor.

2. Your exam score will determine 85% of your final score. The remaining 15% is based on your seniority. Your seniority score is calculated as 70 plus ½ (or .5) point for each three (3) months of completed, permanent (non-provisional) and continuous employment with a job title under the Department of Citywide

Administrative Services. If you have had employment gaps of City employment service of more than one year, no credit is given. Up to a maximum of 15 years is credited for your City service.

Summary:

70+ (.5 point for every 3 months of qualifying City service) =Seniority score

Your final score is calculated based on the following:

(Your multiple choice test score x .85) +(Your seniority score x .15) =Final total score

VACANCIES FOR TRAIN OPERATOR

Since the first Train Operator open competitive exam was administered in 2000, the exam has been offered separately as open competitive and promotional in 2004, 2009, 2016 (promotional only) and 2017 (open competitive only). Eligible transit workers who pass the promotional train operator exam are considered first for vacancies. Once the promotional list of candidates has been exhausted, applicants on the open competitive list are then considered for any remaining vacancies.

The number of applicants filing for this exam has increased significantly in the later years as the popularity of this exam has attracted more candidates. The attractive compensation, uncertain economy, benefits and pension for the union position has attracted both high school and college graduates and those with extensive work experience in other fields. Competition for the train operator position exceeds available vacancies. The number of vacancies in a year for train operator varies depending on many factors, including the number of new train operators failing School Car or being terminated before their one year probationary period, retirements, promotions, demotions, terminations after probationary period (it can happen), resignations, the hiring needs of NYCT and approved headcount by the NYC Office of Management and Budget.

The bottom line is that not everyone who passes the test with a minimum score of seventy percent (70%) will be considered for the position. What this means is that you will need to maximize your score on test day to increase your chances of being called for train operator vacancies.

VACANCIES FOR CONDUCTOR

Vacancies for NYCT Conductor will vary yearly. As discussed in the section above, the number of vacancies depends on many factors, including the number of new conductors failing School Car or being fired before their one year probationary period, retirements, promotions, demotions, terminations after completing probationary period, resignations, the hiring needs of NYCT and approved headcount by the NYC Office of Management and Budget.

Because the qualifications for NYCT Conductor are only a high school diploma or its educational equivalent without any work experience, more applicants file for the Conductor exam than the Train Operator test. The last open competitive Conductor exam administered in 2016 attracted over 45,000 applicants and over 31,000 candidates passed the Conductor open competitive exam. However, not everyone who passes an exam is contacted for a position. This book helps you earn a high score to increase your chances of being contacted for the job.

A retired subway car repurposed for maintenance needs.

3 NYC CIVIL SERVICE

To obtain most positions with the City of New York, New York State Civil Service Law requires candidates to take a competitive civil service exam to be considered for vacancies. The format of civil service exams includes one or a combination of the following:

1. Multiple-choice test
2. Online Education and Experience test
3. Practical test
4. Physical fitness test
5. Psychological assessment

Most New York City civil service exams are in multiple choice format. Taking a civil service exam is the first step in the hiring process with the City. Current city employees are eligible to take promotional exams for their respective job titles. Passing a civil service exam does **not guarantee** a job or a promotion to a higher job title. If you pass a civil service exam, the next step in the hiring process may include, depending on the type of job, a physical exam (eg. law enforcement and labor intensive positions), medical assessment, review of an employee's performance appraisals and attendance record (promotional civil service exams) or participating in hiring pool interviews. If a position is considered safety sensitive, including Bus Operator, Train Operator and Conductor, candidates must take a drug screening test and undergo a FBI background check.

Civil service exams can be administered as both open competitive and promotional for the same job title. Other times only eligible City employees may take a promotional exam for a job title. Provisional city employees are eligible to take a qualifying incumbent exam (QIE) when it's offered for their job title. I will explain provisionals on the next page.

Some City positions do not offer civil service exams, including Attorney, Physician and Research Scientist. These positions are classified as non-competitive in that individuals are not hired through a competitive exam. Applicants submit their cover letter and resume for a job vacancy and are interviewed; similar to the hiring process in the private sector. Employees who are in non-competitive titles should consider taking a civil service exam to secure an underlying civil service title in the event of layoffs.

CIVIL SERVICE ADMINISTRATION

The Department of Citywide Administrative Services (DCAS) administers most civil service exams for the City of New York. NYCT and the Triborough Bridge and Tunnel Authority (TBTA) are responsible for its own civil service exam functions, including writing and administering exams and managing eligible lists. NYCT's Exams Unit is responsible for writing civil service test questions and assembling exams drawn from a computerized test bank. Various personnel assist in writing the test questions, including Test and Measurement Specialists, Train Service Supervisors, Staff Analyst and Associate Staff Analyst employees.

PROVISIONAL vs. PERMANENT EMPLOYEES

Individuals who are employed with the City of New York in a competitive title without taking a civil service exam are considered **provisional** (temporary) employees. Provisional employees mean that individuals were hired for a job with the City from a job interview. This hiring process occurs when no civil service list is available for a job title and a city agency has one or more vacancies for a position. Most city agencies post its jobs on a centralized City jobs website at http://www1.nyc.gov/jobs/index.page or through its agency's website. Applicants upload their cover letter and resume online and if a recruiter or hiring manager is interested, applicants are interviewed for a position.

In accordance with NYS Civil Service Law, provisionals can serve no more than nine (9) months in a competitive position. Provisionals are eventually replaced by individuals that have been appointed from an eligible list as a result of passing a civil service exam in a particular job title. After individuals who are appointed from an eligible list serve a probationary period (varies from 1 year to 2 years), they become permanent with civil service protections. Protections include union representation for probable disciplinary hearings and due process. During infrequent layoffs, provisionals are the first to be laid off followed by permanent civil service employees in reverse seniority order.

NYCT PROVISIONAL EMPLOYEES

NYCT historically has had immediate hiring needs for skilled trades, including Elevator and Escalator Mechanics, Car Inspectors and Signal Maintainers. The eligible civil service lists are usually exhausted quickly, and provisional positions are advertised. Interested applicants apply on the MTA employment website with a cover letter and resume. If an applicant is successful, he/she is appointed as a provisional employee and must take the next civil service exam to be considered permanent after serving a one year probationary period. Failure to take a civil service exam or not passing an exam will result in eventual termination of employment. Your employment time while you are in provisional status is not included in the one year probationary period.

For the positions of train operator and conductor, NYCT has had hired both open competitive candidates and current NYCT employees for provisional positions while waiting for their test scores and list numbers. This occurs when NYCT has an immediate shortage of employees in a job title. For the train operator exam administered in 2017, the top scorers on the open competitive exam were offered provisional train operator positions in 2018 before the release of their list number on the eligible list. The reason behind the provisional appointments was the shortage of train operators from a wave of retirements and numerous employees who did not successfully pass School Car. Individuals who accepted and successfully passed the physical exam and drug screening were hired as provisional train operators. Once provisional employees are appointed from the **eligible list**, they will be reclassified as permanent. The provisional time served as train operator is not included in the one year probationary period.

ELIGIBLE LIST

An eligible list has candidates who have scored at or above a minimum passing score (typically 70%). Candidates are ranked in descending test score order. When applying for a civil service exam, applicants may claim additional points that can be added to a test score, including those who served in the military or are disabled due to active duty. Note that you can only claim veteran points, etc. only once. Government agencies cannot appoint whomever they want and must follow the 1-in-3 rule. For example, the top 3 candidates in score order on the Staff Analyst list are considered for a vacant position. Out of the 3 candidates, candidate #2 is selected for Staff Analyst. Therefore, candidates #1 and #3 are then considered for the next vacancy with candidate #4 on the list. A City agency goes down the eligible list to fill vacancies or to replace provisionals until either the list is exhausted or the eligible list is terminated (typically after four years). Should a candidate be considered and not selected for a position three times by the same agency, that candidate is removed from that agency's list for any future consideration. The agency can (but not required) grant a candidate's written request for later restoration to the list. However, the candidate can be considered by other City agencies for the same title that he/she had passed an exam.

If you are a current City of New York employee, you should ask your city agency if Human Resources has received the certified civil service exam list from DCAS. You should inquire if your agency will reach your list number and if you will be appointed from the list. Should you receive a notice from another city agency that invites you to a hiring pool, you would inform your agency immediately. If your current agency chooses to, Human Resources will give you a "DP-72" form to bring to the hiring pool at another agency. That agency will appoint you on behalf of your current city agency to receive civil service status. However, your current agency must approve the civil service list appointment by giving you the "DP-72" form to bring to the hiring pool.

City agencies may or may not reach everyone on an eligible list. It is in the best interest of a candidate to score as high as possible on an exam. Civil service exams vary in difficulty. Some of the most challenging civil service exams offered by the City of New York, include Associate Staff Analyst and Administrative Staff Analyst. In 2015, approximately 30% of City employees passed the Associate Staff Analyst promotional exam[3].

PURE PROVISIONALS

If you are a current City employee who does not have any civil service title (ie. known as **pure provisional**), I strongly recommend that you take any civil service exam that you qualify for to secure permanent civil service status. Pure provisionals are the first employees to be laid off during budget cuts. They can be bumped from their position and replaced by an individual who is selected from an eligible list or who has permanent civil service status.

To learn more about the civil service process, I recommend the following websites for additional review:

http://www.nyc.gov/html/dcas/html/work/civilservice_1.shtml
http://www.osaunion.org/

ADVICE

Candidates who are interested in a position at the MTA should consider taking any exams that they qualify for. Once you are hired after serving a probationary period, employees can apply for positions internally. Depending on an employee's title, he/she may receive priority in being considered for vacancies before non-Transit employees. For example, Mr. Jones is hired from an open competitive list as a Station Agent and he takes the promotional exam for Conductor. He is considered first for vacancies for Conductor.

Transit employees who want to move to other positions that require technical skills have access to training courses sponsored by the Transport Workers Union Local 100. The union offers civil service test prep courses for its members who are preparing for promotional civil service exams.

---

[3] http://osaunion.org/exam/main.html, Accessed on August 6, 2018

Transit employees who are promoted may return to their previous civil service title within one year of their promotion. For example, a Conductor takes the promotion to Train Operator. During his/her one year as a train operator, you have the option to return to Conductor. Or if the Conductor fails School Car for train operator, he/she will be allowed to return to his former position.

4 THE LIFE OF A TRAIN OPERATOR AND CONDUCTOR

The following link is the most recent job description for train operator from the MTA NYCT's Notice of Examination in December 2016:

http://web.mta.info/nyct/hr/pdf_exams/7604.pdf

Unfortunately, the Notice of Examination for Conductor has been removed from the MTA website. You can view the Notice for the 2008 exam at:

http://www.nyc.gov/html/dcas/downloads/pdf/noes/200808094000.pdf

The job specifications discussed in the Notice gives an applicant a general idea about the job. However, the specifications are far from giving applicants a true understanding and idea of the job. I will discuss different aspects of the job in this chapter.

A number of excellent videos about the job of a train operator are available on YouTube. The first link is an interview with a NYCT train operator and the second link is interviews with train operators who work for the Bay Area Rapid Transit (BART) subway system.

https://www.youtube.com/watch?v=_0nw5C7hHOQ

https://www.youtube.com/watch?v=kD9Wks3bZSM&t=49s

COMPENSATION AND BENEFITS

When train operators are hired, new employees will be appointed to the Train Operator (Yard) title. Employees are guaranteed a 40-hour work week. As of February 2018, Train Operator (Yard) pays $34.8275 per hour, or $72,441 per year. After 231 days of operating trains in passenger service, your title will change to Train Operator (Road) and earn the maximum rate of $36.25 per hour, or $75,400 per year.

Conductors are compensated at the maximum hourly rate of $31.635 per hour over a 40-hour work week, or $65,801 per year. However, it takes six (6) years for a Conductor to earn the maximum hourly rate. Conductors receive incremental increases in their hourly rate on their work anniversary until their sixth year of employment as follows (rounded to the nearest hundredth):

1st year: 70% of top hourly rate at $22.14
2nd year: 75% of top hourly rate at $23.73

3rd year: 80% of top hourly rate at $25.31
4th year: 85% of top hourly rate at $26.89
5th year: 90% of top hourly rate at $28.47
6th year: 100% of top hourly rate at $31.64

Operators and conductors receive night and weekend differential pay (ie. additional compensation for working during nights and weekends), holiday pay and both mandatory (ie. forced overtime) and voluntary overtime.

Employees accrue vacation and sick time and receive a comprehensive benefits package. Your health insurance is effective on the first day of a month following ninety (90) days of employment with NYCT. City employees can choose a wide range of health insurance plans. The health insurance and defined contribution retirement programs (voluntary payroll deductions into your government retirement plan) are administered by the Office of Labor Relations (OLR). Visit its website at www.nyc.gov/olr to review benefits in detail.

DEFINED BENEFIT PENSION

NYCT employees receive a defined benefit pension plan, and they are vested into their pension after ten (10) years of service. Defined benefit pensions are increasingly rare in the private sector. Defined benefit pensions are based on a formula to determine a retirement amount that an employee will receive when he/she qualifies for a pension. The pension amount is calculated based on length of service and 3-year average highest salary earned at the time of retirement. Your pension received is not effected by the financial performance of pension money invested into the financial markets.

Your pension plan is administered by the New York City Employees Retirement System (NYCERS). New hires enter into the Tier 6 pension plan; unless you had previous City of New York service under a previous tier. If this is the case, you might be able to buy back your previous years of City service for credit under a previous tier that you had entered during City employment. There are exceptions and you will need to check with your union or NYCERS.

NYCT employees qualify for a full pension with twenty-five (25) years of service in the Transit Authority **and** at age fifty-five (55).

For the City of New York's defined benefit pension plan for Tier 6, kindly go to the following website that gives further details: www.nycers.org

WORKING CONDITIONS

Train operators and conductors work in an enclosed train cab. This subway cab is the R160, a new technology train (NTT) model used in the B Division (lettered routes).

Train Operators and Conductors work in a noisy industrial environment with heavy machinery and equipment. Employee and passenger safety are important in the mass transportation industry. The train operator and conductor titles are represented positions with the Transport Workers Union Local 100. The union negotiates, among others, with MTA Labor Relations on working conditions, compensation for its TWU members within NYCT and represents non-probationary employees at disciplinary hearings.

Another class of train operators is Locomotive Engineers who are employed with the Staten Island Railway, Long Island Railroad and Metro North Railroad. These Engineers are represented by the Brotherhood of Locomotive Engineers (BLE).

The Metropolitan Transportation Authority (MTA) is a 24-hour 7 days a week operation. Train operators and conductors are needed wherever and whenever based on NYCT's needs of the service. Train operators and conductors who complete School Car training will find themselves working on different subway lines. But as one gains seniority they will be able to pick a relatively predictable shift. It may take decades of service before train operators and conductors are able to pick weekends off. Senior employees tend to pick Saturdays and Sundays as their regular days off (RDOs).

Train operators and conductors have two picks per year to select their job assignments in seniority order. Employees who are unable to pick are known as road extra or extra extras. Extras can have their tour of duty changed by the train crew office among AM (4:00 AM-11:59 AM), PM (12 PM to 9:59 PM) or Midnight (10 PM to 3:59 AM) tours. Note that military time is used at Transit.

Train operators and conductors work alone for prolonged periods in an enclosed train cab that is separated from passengers. Train operators and conductors are prohibited from listening to music, looking at their phones or engaged in any distractions while on duty. Train operators can face dismissal from employment if they are seen using their phones while operating their trains.

Train operators and conductors face challenges with balancing their personal lives, including child care needs, attending school and other responsibilities. Candidates who are seriously considering the train operator or conductor position should have a conversation with his/her family about the potential impact that the job will have in their lives.

JOB SPECIFICATIONS

Train operators and conductors travel throughout NYC's four boroughs (Manhattan, Brooklyn, Queens and Bronx) at different times of a day. Train operators and conductors do not work on Staten Island. The Staten Island Railway is a separate system, and operates its own trains with federally certified locomotive engineers and conductors. Where you report to work is called reporting locations and your job assignment may take you to the outer boroughs that involve considerable travel time. The train crew office will try to give you reporting locations close to your home as agreed and enshrined in the union contract, but this is not guaranteed.

Your reporting locations are determined by the Subdivision you were either able to pick or assigned during School Car. Subdivision A includes the number lines and Times Square Shuttle and Subdivision B are the letter lines. Most reporting locations for Subdivision A are in the Bronx or upper Manhattan (an exception is the Flushing 7 line that operates between Manhattan and Queens with its Corona train yard in Flushing, Queens), while Subdivision B has reporting locations mostly in Brooklyn and Queens. Subdivision C is the construction and work trains, etc., which are picked by senior train operators who have received additional training to operate specialized equipment.

Train operators and conductors carry heavy equipment and tools for them to perform their job duties, including radio, earmuffs, brake handle (for train operators), gas mask, keys, Book of Rules, etc. The job can be physically taxing and train operators and conductors need to stay awake during train operation; despite working at different hours of a day and operating on different subway routes. While on duty, employees are prohibited from taking naps even when they are not operating trains. Train operators and conductors are not allowed to sleep in crew rooms or within Transit property. Disciplinary action can be taken on employees who fail to abide.

Operators and conductors are exposed to the elements both underground and aboveground. For example, walking to an outdoor train yard during a rainstorm to prepare a train for passenger service and being held beyond his/her tour of duty during snow emergencies. Train operators and conductors regularly step over live third rails (600 volts that power the NYC subway system) and walk on cat walks in tunnels and on elevated tracks that may be hundreds of feet above a street. Some new hires during School Car have quit when they learn that these tasks are part of the job responsibilities. If possible, take a leave of absence from your current job to see if being a train operator or conductor is the right career for you.

TRAIN OPERATION RESPONSIBILITIES

Train operators manipulate the throttle and brake handle to control the speed and braking of their subway train. Operators must safely handle their trains into stations efficiently and safely. They manipulate buttons on the control panel to enable the conductor to open and to close the train doors on the correct side of a platform on the new technology trains (NTT). During **one person train operation** (OPTO) without a conductor on board, train operators are responsible for operating their train, opening and closing the train doors at station stops and setting up the automatic announcement system on the **train operator display** (TOD) or to make manual announcements on the older trains. Operators may interact with their passengers during service delays and changes. On computer driven trains that are in **automatic train operation** (ATO), train operators push the ATO start button to depart at each station and respond accordingly to commands on the TOD.

Operators monitor the subway tracks for any hazards, monitor the tracks and platforms for any passengers who are dangerously close to the train, anticipate incorrect track switches that may direct a train on to a wrong track, respond and to distinguish color signals (aspects) (eg. train signals, flags, lanterns) that regulate the movement of a train. Some examples include lanterns and/or flags set up to warn train operators of track personnel on the roadbed (tracks) ahead, interpreting numerous signals and signs that govern train movement on particular sections of track.

With additional training, Train Operators can qualify to operate work trains in Subdivision C that include both electric and diesel locomotives. Train operators are exposed to diesel fumes and the hot and cold weather for prolonged periods. These jobs usually contain a lot of overtime and have no interaction with passengers.

Train Operators are required to take a refresher course every three years and train on a subway simulator. Instructors will simulate various scenarios on the computer screen for train operators to respond to in a mock train operator cab.

Although Train Operators work solo after completing School Car, they are subjected to random inspections by Train Service Supervisors that critique their operation. Superintendents may evaluate train crew performance. Undercover Transit investigators (known as beakies) may ride the trains to monitor train crew compliance with the Book of Rules and Transit directives. Train operators may supervise School Car train operators and instruct them on train operation during their shifts.

Other aspects of the job include (not an exhaustive list):

- Investigates his/her assigned train going into brakes-in-emergency that involve inspecting a train for the cause (including walking around his/her train in a tunnel and on elevated tracks and descending in between subway cars to inspect);
- Walks in dimly lit subway tunnels with a flashlight and safety vest or on elevated tracks to retrieve and to prepare trains for service in underground storage yards and elevated train yards with potential tripping hazards;
- Performs a pre-trip safety inspection check before operating a train in passenger service
- Walks near the electrified third rail, along the catwalk and with subway traffic running on adjacent tracks;
- Prepares incident reports of unusual occurrences to train supervision;
- Maintains communication with the Rail Control Center (RCC) console dispatchers and other train dispatchers through two-way radio, telephone, etc.;
- Receives orders from RCC that may impact train service (eg. bypassing local stations when an express train is rerouted on the local track);
- Cooperates, communicates and works with different Conductors;
- Interacts with a Road Car Inspector (RCI) during equipment failure;
- Brings a train to car washes with potential exposure to chemicals that require wearing protective gear;
- Operates a train to a barn for repairs and maintenance;
- Moves trains to storage tracks and train yards not needed for passenger service (known as a lay up);
- Couples and decouples subway cars
- Exposure to steel dust, diesel fumes and other particles;

- Submits to random drug and alcohol tests throughout your Transit career, including promotions and incidents (eg. passenger injury and derailments);
- Operates inside an enclosed train cab that requires extended sitting or standing during train operation;
- Experiences time pressure from Train Dispatchers and Rail Control Center to operate trains and to achieve on-time train performance
- Wears earmuffs to reduce the likelihood of hearing loss from a noisy industrial environment of the screeching of trains
- Witnesses and responds to 12-9s (ie. passenger under train), inspects whether a passenger is alive or deceased and reports back to RCC;
- Testifies in depositions, civil lawsuits and criminal trials and investigations;
- Gives testimony as a result of derailments and accidents to NYC Transit, state and federal investigators (eg. National Transportation Safety Board);
- Cooperates with the MTA Inspector General during audits and investigations;
- Ascends and descends to/from trains, platforms, catwalks, etc.;
- Wears a uniform required of all train operators;
- Perform platform duties while on restricted duty, including facilitating the timely movement of trains out of stations, ensuring passengers are off a train at terminals, and answering passengers' questions and
- Performs jobs/duties as assigned by train supervision (known as work as assigned)

CONDUCTOR RESPONSIBILITIES

Road conductors who work on trains make manual announcements to customers, including station stops, transfer information, delays and emergencies. On the new technology trains, conductors set up the automatic announcement system (AAS). They answer passenger questions, including giving points of interest and directions. Conductors communicate with their train operator, train supervision and the Rail Control Center.

The most important responsibility of conductors is to point at the conductor's indication board (a zebra striped board) when the train is fully berthed into the station. If the Conductor is not facing the conductor's board, the Conductor must not open the train doors since the train cars are most likely not facing the platform for passengers to enter and to exit the train safely. Since platforms can be on either side of the train, conductors must open the train doors on the correct side of a train. Conductors must check and adjust the destination and route signs on their train. Incorrect signs on a train could subject a train crew to disciplinary action.

After closing the train doors, the Conductor must extend his/her head out of the cab window to observe the train and to ensure no passengers are being dragged while the train leaves the station. Train Service Supervisors will observe Conductors to ensure that these tasks are being performed, or face disciplinary action.

Other conductors may elect to become construction flaggers who set up flags and light signals to protect workers who are doing work on or near the subway tracks. Conductors may work as platform conductors in stations that involve patrolling platforms, assist customers in entering and exiting trains, answer questions from passengers, ensure passengers leave the train at terminal stations and assist in the timely dispatch of trains. Conductors who work in subway yards manipulate hand-thrown switches for train movement. They are involved with ensuring that the track switches are clear of any obstructions.

WORK RELATED STRESS

Train operators and conductors encounter unruly passengers that may be verbally or physically abusive, deal with emergencies under considerable stress (eg. evacuation of a train during power failure, derailments, witnesses a crime). Train operators and conductors encounter the homeless and panhandlers frequently and the number of homeless riding the subway or in stations increases substantially during cold weather. Conductors can be assaulted when they lean out their cab window to observe the platform and train.

One of the most stressful part of the position is encountering passenger and employee fatalities. Almost all subway and railroad crews will encounter passenger suicides and accidents during their career. In most cases, train operators will encounter individuals jumping in front of their train. The inevitable part of being a train operator is the ability to cope after a tragic event, develop strategies to overcome potential post-traumatic stress, seek counseling services and to return to work mentally prepared. Train operators are given three days off if a fatality occurs. Some train operators do not return to work and with a pay cut, they can go on disability. Other operators may choose to return to their former title (eg. Conductor) or resign.

The following is a YouTube video that gives insights into NYCT train operators who experience tragedy on the tracks: https://www.youtube.com/watch?v=Iih1-MRe_LE. It is important that applicants understand that these events are inevitably part of the train operator job.

PROMOTIONAL OPPORTUNITIES FOR TRAIN OPERATORS

Train operators have multiple avenues of promotional opportunities in **Rapid Transit Operations** (RTO), including supervisory titles as Train Service Supervisor (TSS) and Train Dispatcher (TD). Train operators must have been in their position for two years before being promoted to TSS. There are five different specialties within the TSS position. Transit will review your work attendance history (including your sick time use), performance evaluation and disciplinary record as factors to be considered for promotion. Employees who have used sixty-seven (67%) percent of their sick time may be automatically disqualified from promotion. As with passing a civil service exam, promotions are not guaranteed.

Transit employees who are being considered for promotion should check with Human Resources that the office has your latest performance evaluation. Employees may risk being passed over for consideration if their file is incomplete. Employees who promote to a higher title may return to their previous position within one year. For example, a Bus Operator who accepts the promotion to Train Operator can return to his/her Bus Operator position within one year. Human Resources may ask you to write a G-2 to explain why you are resigning your promotional title to return to your former position.

From TD or TSS, additional promotional opportunities without further civil service examination include Console Dispatcher at the Rail Control Center in midtown Manhattan or Superintendent who oversees a particular area of the subway system.

Train Operators are eligible to apply for other internal positions with one year of service including Dedicated Announcer. Dedicated Announcers give status updates involving train delays and rerouted service and recommend alternative routes. Announcers obtain incident related information from the RCC and translate the information that is clear and understandable to passengers.

PROMOTIONAL OPPORTUNITIES FOR CONDUCTORS

Conductors have promotional opportunities in RTO. They can take the promotional exams for Train Operator, Tower Operator and Assistant Train Dispatcher. They must have completed their one year probationary period when they are appointed for a promotional title.

Conductors are eligible to apply for other internal positions with one year of service including Dedicated Announcer. Dedicated Announcers give status updates involving train delays and rerouted service and recommend alternative routes. Announcers obtain incident related information from the RCC and translate the information that is clear and understandable to passengers.

LOCOMOTIVE ENGINEER OPPORTUNITIES

Occasionally, the MTA announces openings for Locomotive Engineer at the Long Island Railroad (LIRR) and Metro North Railroad (MNR). Usually individuals who are eligible to apply are federally certified locomotive engineers from other railroad systems or current LIRR and MNR employees eligible for promotion. However, in recent years the LIRR and MNR have considered Train Operators and Bus Operators for vacancies. If you are interested in railroad opportunities, gaining experience as a Train Operator may be an excellent stepping stone to becoming a Locomotive Engineer. Other regional railroads, including New Jersey Transit and Port Authority Trans Hudson (PATH), consider train operators to fill its vacancies for Locomotive Engineer.

Locomotive Engineers with the LIRR and MNR are paid significantly more than NYCT Train Operators, but the training process is intense and long. In contrast to NYCT Train Operators, Locomotive Engineers are required to learn hundreds of signals and definitions (S&D) and write them exactly on the S&D test and memorize the physical characteristics of the railroad system (eg. Track switches, tracks, speed limits, signals, etc.) In recent years, locomotive engineers have left New Jersey Transit to work for LIRR and MNR that offer competitive hourly wages.

Vacancies for locomotive engineers are posted under the Employment page at www.mta.info

NO RESIDENCY REQUIREMENT

Most civil service positions with the City of New York require that you initially be a New York City resident of the five boroughs. After two years of City employment, employees can reside in the surrounding suburbs of New York State and Long Island. However, train operators and conductors do not have a residency requirement, and employees can live in any state. Transit employees are required to report to work on time regardless of where one resides. Employees who travel to work in private vehicles are discouraged.

An R188 subway train on the Flushing 7 line that is in automatic train operation (ATO). The only other subway line in ATO is the L line. The lines use the Communications Based Train Control (CBTC) system.

5 THE HIRING PROCESS

The hiring process has changed considerably since the previous administration of the 2009 open competitive train operator exam and the 2008 open competitive conductor exam. For the 2016 and 2017 open competitive conductor and train operator exams, candidates are required to take an Oral Proficiency Assessment (OPA) that has two parts; assessing their ability to memorize and to recall facts and candidates' proficiency in English. For example, candidates hear an audio conversation between a train operator and the Rail Control Center. Applicants are then asked to recall what they have heard by answering multiple choice questions. The second part of the OPA is a two personal panel that shows both visuals for a response and the examiners ask scenario related questions to candidates. A candidate's responses are recorded on audio equipment. You need at least 70% to pass the OPA to continue the hiring process. Some candidates may receive letters to take the OPA before receiving their test scores. Candidates will be notified at a later date if they have passed the OPA. Once candidates are placed on an eligible list after the answer key is finalized and the tests are scored, Human Resources contacts candidates in list order number for further processing as vacancies occur.

INTERVIEW DAY FOR TRAIN OPERATOR AND CONDUCTOR

After the release of the open competitive eligible list for train operator or conductor, the length of time that NYCT contacts candidates varies. Factors include candidates who decline the position, candidates who are disqualified including certain criminal offenses committed, unsatisfactory driving record (train operator only), medical issues and trainees who fail School Car and are terminated. It is important that test takers keep their contact information up-to-date, as Transit will send your exam results to the mailing address on file. Once your name is reached on the eligible list, NYC Transit will mail you a letter with the date and time to report for your "interview."

It is recommended that you arrive before the scheduled time so you can complete the processing quickly. Bring a bottle of water and some snacks as there will be a lot of waiting. You will encounter applicants for other positions and Transit employees who are there for drug testing and other paperwork.

You should respond to the letter if you decline the position. In accordance to Civil Service Law, you can decline a maximum of three times before your name is removed permanently from the list for further consideration. Each time you decline, you will need to write NYCT to restore your name on to the eligible list.

COMPREHENSIVE PERSONNEL DOCUMENT

On interview day, an applicant reports to Human Resources at 180 Livingston Street in Brooklyn and receives a thick booklet (**Comprehensive Personnel Document- CPD**). The CPD asks you to list all of your residential addresses, employment history since high school, any unemployment periods and how you supported yourself, educational history, any arrests/convictions, etc. On the same day, a candidate will give a urine sample that will be tested for drugs and alcohol. The drug test results are valid for thirty (30) days. If an applicant does not receive an email within that time frame for the next processing step, he/she may be asked to submit another urine sample.

It is important that the CPD booklet is completed accurately and truthfully at home. Any intentional withholding of information can result in immediate termination. Background investigations are done by an independent contractor for the MTA and can take up to a year to complete, and applicants who are found to have intentionally falsified information on their employment application are terminated. Terminations have occurred during and after completing School Car. Arrests and/or convictions should be disclosed (bring your disposition papers) and any outstanding summonses and fines settled before the hiring process. Keep all your receipts as proof that you paid your fines in full. You should consider bringing your mobile device in case Human Resources notifies you of any unpaid tickets. You can settle the fines on the spot and show the representative proof on your phone that it has been paid.

If you have held multiple jobs and do not recall your employment history, you can contact your Social Security Office to obtain a Social Security Earnings Information report. The form number for the report is the SSA-7050-F4 and you want to request a non-certified detailed earnings information. This option gives the periods of employment or self-employment and the names and addresses of employers on the report. There is a fee for this report, and you may want to contact your local Social Security office to determine if you can expedite the report.

With the motor vehicle license requirement for train operator, NYCT will review your NYS Department of Motor Vehicles driver abstract. Any moving violations or serious accidents may disqualify you from further consideration for Train Operator.

NEXT STEPS AFTER INTERVIEW

If you pass the urine toxicology test, you will receive an email asking you to come in for a medical screening and possibly final human resource processing. Final processing occurs if there is an opening in an upcoming training class. Make sure that you add NYCT's email address to your contact list to avoid any email going into your spam folder.

Your medical test consists of completing a questionnaire that details your health history, including any medications that you take. You will be tested for your physical strength, blood pressure, EKG, vision and hearing to determine if you can perform the essential duties of train operator or conductor. Train operators will be tested for sleep apnea. Candidates should have the telephone number of their physician available. If you have a medical condition, Transit may require your physician to complete a form for submission to the Medical Assessment Center (MAC). For example, a diabetic candidate may obtain a doctor's letter stating that his/her diabetes is being controlled by medication and he/she is able to perform the job. If you are not able to resolve everything with the Medical Department, you will be placed on medical hold and you will miss the next training class. Certain medical conditions may disqualify a candidate if it interferes with the essential duties of the job (eg. a history of seizures).

Final processing involves meeting a human resources specialist that will review your personnel file with you (**bring your completed CPD**), ask you to clarify any discrepancies, and if the review is satisfactory you will be sworn in. A picture is taken for your employee pass, enrollment into the NYC employee pension system (NYCERS) and an information packet is given on the details of where and when to report on your first day of employment.

FIRST WEEK FOR NEW HIRES

New hires attend orientation and both NYC Transit's Human Resources and the TWU-Local 100 union reviews employee benefits on the first day. Your second day of employment will determine where you will be going; Subdivision A (number lines and Grand Central shuttle train) or Subdivision B (letter lines). Your list number from the eligible list will determine your seniority in picking which subdivision you want to work in. It is not guaranteed that you have a choice. Sometimes the entire class will be assigned to Subdivision A or B, or the class will be split between the two subdivisions. New hires will pick their pay location; to receive your biweekly paycheck and your W2. To avoid the hassle, enroll in direct deposit to have your pay deposited into your bank account.

You will be measured for your uniforms and receive Transit approved footwear before accessing the subway tracks. During the end of the first week, new hires will likely report to the Learning Center in south Brooklyn to begin their training. New hires will be split into smaller classes and you will meet your TSS instructors to learn the position and to complete School Car training.

6 EXAM INFORMATION

PRE-TEST DAY

The MTA releases its upcoming civil service exam schedule on its website around June of each year at http://web.mta.info/nyct/hr/index_nyct_employment.html. The schedule lists the job titles and the application dates for each exam. Sometimes exams may be cancelled or postponed to a later date. It is a good idea to check the website at the beginning of each month. When the Train Operator or Conductor Notice of Examination is published, read the entire Notice to understand and to determine if you qualify to take the exam. You will need to create an online account with the MTA to enable you to file for the exam and to apply for other civil service exams and jobs throughout the MTA. The exam application will ask you to complete a basic profile of yourself, including name, mailing address, etc. that will be submitted to take the test.

After you file and pay for the Train Operator or Conductor test (debit or credit card is accepted), the MTA website will post updates regarding the exam date(s) and when you will receive your admissions exam letter in the mail. If you need testing accommodations due to a disability or religious observances, be sure to follow the instructions outlined in the Notice of Examination and/or application form. If you don't receive your exam letter by a certain date (about 10 days before the first exam date), the website directs you to go to the MTA Exam Information Center with a date, time and location. NYCT will generally try to assign you to a testing site that is in the borough that you reside based on your mailing address. It is recommended that you apply for the exam as soon as possible.

Read the admissions letter carefully with what you can and cannot bring to the testing site. Take note of the test date (morning or afternoon session), testing site's address and public transportation to get to the site. And consider visiting the testing site on the day of the week that you will take the test to simulate how long it will take to travel. You may not be able to see actual room that you will sit for the exam, but you can familiarize yourself with the building and its surroundings.

You will need to bring at least the following:

- a government issued identification card (I recommend your driver's license)
- NYC Transit employee identification (for **promotional exam** only)
- a non-smart watch to keep track of your time during the test
- basic non-scientific calculator that has addition, subtraction, division and multiplication functions (calculators on any type of phone are not allowed)
- No. 2 pencils with eraser
- a bottle of water (drink sparingly during the test)

You will need to complete some forms on test day for the open competitive exam. The information that you will need to give includes a state issued driver identification number (train operator exam only), the name of your employer that meets the one-year continuous work experience with one employer (train operator exam only) and to confirm that you possess a high school diploma or its educational equivalent. This information is completed on a scannable sheet that will be provided on test day.

TEST DAY

On the day of the exam, expect a long line of candidates waiting outside a public high school to enter the testing site. Arrive on time or you will not be allowed to take the exam if you are late. Test proctors and/or security personnel will ask to see your admissions exam letter and identification card before entry into the building. Be sure that you have your NYCT admissions exam letter, as a number of candidates showed up without the letter! When you approach the entrance of a public school, a test proctor will give you a card directing you to the classroom to take your test. Once you are in the assigned classroom, you will need to choose a seat to sit for the exam. Be mindful it the exam is in the winter and you are seated near a radiator or near a window if a game is occurring.

Candidates are given a **Candidate's Record of Answers** sheet for them to enter all of their answers to the test questions. This is the only document that you can take with you after the exam is finished. Candidates are not given extra time to record their answers either on the computerized answer sheet that serves as their official answers submitted for scoring or the Candidate's Record of Answers. Candidates receive a separate scannable sheet to complete their high school education, driver's license (train operator exam only) and employment information (train operator exam only). A one-page scrap paper is included with the test booklet to give extra space for you to write on. Any answers on the scrap paper or the test booklet are not scored and must be returned at the end of the test. You are allowed to write on your test booklet.

Candidates will hear three bells during the exam. The first bell will signal your test proctor to read the instructors that assist you in completing the forms and procedures that govern the administration of the exam. Once I was seated at my desk I began to complete the forms. I used the first bell to relax and to listen to the proctor for anything that I may have missed when completing the forms. The second bell signals the beginning of the train operator or conductor test. For the train operator exam, candidates can now open their test booklets to begin the 2.5-hour exam (open competitive) or 3-hour exam (promotional). For the conductor exam, the exam is 3 hours for both open competitive and promotional. The third bell informs all candidates that the test has concluded. You should keep track of your time and make the necessary preparations to transfer all your answers on to the official answer sheet before the third bell. During the test, a proctor will take each candidate's fingerprints.

Candidates are allowed to leave before the test time limit. Gather your personal belongings and follow the instructions from your proctor on how you should turn in your test when you have finished. You will need to return your test booklet, scannable forms and scrap paper. Be sure to have the proctor sign off on your Candidate's Record of Answers as this is the only ticket to attend the optional protest session. Once you are given the approval to leave, exit the testing site quietly and do not linger inside or you could be disqualified from the exam.

A proposed answer key is released a number of weeks after the last exam session is completed on the MTA civil service employment web page http://web.mta.info/nyct/hr/appexam.htm. Candidates can compare their answers marked on their Record of Answers against the proposed answer key to determine their preliminary score.

Do not even think about cheating on the exam. You will be escorted off the testing site, your test score invalidated and banned from City employment for a number of years. You could potentially face criminal prosecution.

PROTEST SESSION

A non-mandatory protest session is scheduled for applicants who want to protest any test questions that they believe their answer was correct and/or better than the proposed answers in the preliminary answer key. Candidates are told of the date, time and location to report to the protest session. On the day of the protest session, an employee will give you the test booklet based on the test date and AM or PM session that you completed the exam. During the time allowed, you can examine the test questions and review the questions that you answered incorrectly based on the proposed answer key. Candidates may submit documentation to support their assertion. Written protests to test questions can either be made at the session or by mail postmarked no more than thirty days from the protest session date.

A Test Validation Board (TVB) is convened that is composed of a union official, Transit representative and other concerned parties to review all protests submitted. The TVB is empowered by NYS Civil Service Law to allow multiple answers to a test question and to invalidate any test question. Once a final answer key is established for exam, all applicants who met the minimum qualifications as stated in the Notice of Examination receive their exam results; test score and list number (rank number in score order on the eligible list).

UP-TO-DATE ADDRESS

Keep your address up-to-date. If you move, you will not receive future correspondences from NYCT. You will need to submit a Correction Form to update your contact information or correct any inaccuracies with your contact information. The form is available on the MTA's employment website under NYCT employment.

SPECIAL NOTE ON THE TRAIN OPERATOR AND CONDUCTOR EXAMS

Both the train operator and conductor exams overlap in the content and types of questions tested. If you are sitting for the train operator exam, take the train operator test in Chapter 7. Candidates who are taking the conductor exam should complete questions in Chapter 7 and answer the conductor test questions in Chapter 8.

CONTENT AND STRUCTURE OF THE TRAIN OPERATOR EXAM

The 2017 open competitive train operator exam was administered as a multiple choice test that contained sixty (60) questions with a time limit of 2.5 hours. In the past, the open competitive exam had seventy (70) questions with a time limit of 3 hours. The promotional train operator exam consists of eighty (80) questions that are completed in 3 hours.

The exam does **not** assume previous knowledge of the NYC subway system or anything transit related. Therefore, test takers should answer questions based on the information given on the exam and not rely on outside knowledge. Do not overthink the test questions and answers.

The train operator test for both open competitive and promotional consist of primarily reading comprehension and math questions.   Within the reading comprehension questions, background information is given to answer the multiple choice questions. This may include Transit directives, diagrams, maps, policies, procedures or reading passages. Candidates should have the ability to read and to understanding written material in English and solve arithmetic questions in word problem format.

The exam does not test your writing or grammatical skills, any math topics beyond arithmetic or vocabulary.

The exam has a variety of questions that may include:

1. reading passages that describe a set of procedures followed in order, directives issued to transit employees or policies followed by questions,

2. situational questions that require you to take the best course of action or exercise safe and responsible judgment (eg. What action should you take when youths are riding on top of a subway car?),

3. reordering sentences (scrambled paragraphs) that describe an event chronologically and logically to prepare an incident report to train supervision,

4. selecting the best summary that accurately and completely describes a number of facts or observations contained in an employee's report,

5. reading a map or diagram and answering questions based on the visual (eg. reading the layout of a train yard),

6. performing basic mathematical calculations, including addition, subtraction, division, multiplication and computing averages (the format of these questions is usually word problems involving one or a combination of arithmetic operations),

7. calculating the distances between sign markings found in stations or in tunnels,

8. understanding and applying radio codes and its meaning to scenarios,

9. understanding and applying buzzer or train horn signals and its meaning to scenarios and

10. understanding and calculating military time.

You will have multiple opportunities to practice the types of questions described above in Chapter 7. Chapter 7 contains a full length train operator exam that closely follows the format, difficulty level and style of the questions administered from previous exams. The format of the real exam does not follow a particular order in the types of questions presented. For example, math questions and reordering sentences appear randomly throughout the exam.

CONTENT AND STRUCTURE OF THE CONDUCTOR EXAM

Both of the 2016 open competitive and promotion to conductor exams contained seventy (70) questions with a time limit of 3 hours. Before the 2016 conductor exam, previous conductor exams tested New York City points of interest and military time. Candidates were expected to know, for example, what borough is Yankees Stadium located or calculate military time to arrive at an answer. Although these topics were not tested on the 2016 Conductor exam, I have included test questions on these topics in the event that NYCT's Exams Unit decides to include them in future exams.

The exam does **not** assume previous knowledge of the NYC subway system or anything transit related. Therefore, test takers should answer questions based on the information given on the exam and not rely on outside knowledge. Do not overthink the test questions and answers.

The open competitive and promotion to conductor tests consist of primarily reading comprehension, reading and understanding maps and schedules. Within the reading comprehension questions, background information is given to answer the multiple choice questions. This may include Transit bulletins, maps, diagrams, policies, procedures or reading passages. Maps showing different subway routes will appear on the exam and test takers will need to answer questions based on a map. Train schedules frequently appear on past exams.

The exam does not test your writing or grammatical skills, any math topics beyond arithmetic or vocabulary.

The exam has a variety of questions that may include:

1. reading passages that describe a set of procedures followed in order, directives issued to transit employees or policies followed by questions,

2. situational questions that require you to take the best course of action or exercise safe and responsible judgment (eg. What action should you take when youths are riding on top of a subway car?),

3. reordering sentences (scrambled paragraphs) that describe an event chronologically and logically to prepare an incident report to train supervision,

4. selecting the best summary that accurately and completely describes a number of facts or observations contained in an employee's report,

5. reading a map, schedule or diagram and answering questions based on the visual (eg. A portion of a subway map),

6. performing basic mathematical calculations, including addition, subtraction, division, multiplication and computing averages (the format of these questions is usually word problems involving one or a combination of arithmetic operations),

7. understanding and applying radio codes and its meaning to scenarios,

8. understanding and applying buzzer or train horn signals and its meaning to scenarios

9. answering New York City points of interest questions and

10. understanding and calculating military time.

TEST TAKING STRATEGIES

Below are tips to approach the test effectively. Specific strategies to answer the types of questions encountered on the train operator and conductor exams will be given in the explanations to the test questions in Chapters 7 and 8.

- Use the test time limit wisely and **answer the easy reading comprehension questions that contain shorter reading passages and math questions first.** The train operator and conductor exams are paper tests, so you have the freedom to skip around to different questions.

- After tackling the easy questions, focus your remaining time on the hard questions with extensive reading content. This will build your confidence and earn points toward your final score. All questions are worth the same points.

- When skipping questions, keep track of where you mark the answers on the computerized answer sheet. It's very easy to skip question 5 and when answering question 6 to fill in your answer on question 5. **Pay attention!**

- For questions that contain reading passages, directives or procedures, **read each question first** and then scan for the information that is relevant to a test question.

- Do not waste time reading the entire passage. The test questions typically focus on small pieces of information within the long reading passages

- There is **no penalty** for guessing. There are four (4) answer choices for each question. If you are able to eliminate answer choices that do not make sense, you increase the chances of selecting a correct answer. If the test is about to end, randomly choose answers for the remaining unanswered test questions and mark them on your answer sheet. **Do not leave any question unanswered! Each test question is worth the same number of points toward your exam score.**

- Predict and paraphrase what an answer to a question could be. This may seem counterproductive, but reading questions often contain answer choices that are similar. As you read each answer choice, you could be distracted or confused with selecting the best answer to a question. Instead of falling into this trap, cover the answer choices and determine your own answer. Then locate the answer choice that is closest to your answer.

- The test makers like to insert answer choices that look similar but are wrong. For example, the answer to a question is 12:32 PM and two of the incorrect answer choices are 12:23 PM and 12:32 AM. Answer choices may have the same sentences, but a word is changed from northbound to southbound.

- Pay attention to what a question is asking you and beware of answer choices that are designed for individuals who misread a question or answer choice

- Don't overuse your calculator to solve math questions. The questions are designed to test your math skills and the ability to identify a problem and to compute an answer accurately.

- Remember to record your answers on the Candidate's Record of Answers and have the bottom of the sheet signed by the test proctor. This sheet is the only proof that will allow you entry into the protest session and to determine your preliminary test score before you receive your official results in the mail.

STUDY STRATEGIES

- Work on the test questions at the same time and day of your scheduled test.

- Take the test under strict timing conditions. Do not give yourself extra time for the test.

- Review the results of your test. Identify your strengths and weaknesses from your performance on the reading comprehension and math questions.

If math is an area for improvement, I recommend creating an account with Khan Academy (www.khanacademy.org) to access its rich and abundant free math lessons either through its website or Khan Academy app. Your focus should be on the arithmetic lessons; addition, subtraction, multiplication, division, percentages and averages. You may consider choosing a math textbook that has preferably arithmetic word problems to solve.

If reading is an area for improvement, I recommend reading non-fiction books, high quality newspapers and magazines (eg. Bloomberg Businessweek or the New York Times), user manuals or other written material that contain policies, steps or procedures to follow. Quiz yourself and answer the following: (1) the author's main point; (2) key ideas in the reading and (3) summarize the reading.

- Keep practicing the test questions in this book, read daily and practice solving arithmetic word problems

FREQUENTLY ASKED QUESTION (FAQ)

Q: Where can I obtain past copies of Train Operator and Conductor civil service exam questions?

A: Unfortunately, New York City Transit and the City of New York does not release past open competitive and promotional civil service exams. Many decades ago, the City did release previously administered Motorman and Conductor exams. However, the exams contain outdated questions that do not accurately reflect the difficulty level and the content of today's exams. Additionally, the agency does not license nor sell its questions to any test preparation company.

If you desire to practice additional civil service test questions that test reading comprehension and math, I recommend the NYS Department of Civil Service website that offers a number of specific exam prep study guides (https://www.cs.ny.gov/testing/testguides.cfm).

7 TRAIN OPERATOR EXAM

This chapter contains a full length train operator exam that has eighty (80) multiple choice questions designed to be completed in three (3) hours. Based on the 2017 open competitive exam, you can elect to complete the first sixty questions in 2 hours and 30 minutes. For Transit employees who are sitting for the promotional exam, complete all eighty (80) questions with a time limit of three (3) hours.

To maximize the usefulness of this book, I strongly recommend that you eventually complete all of the questions. At the time of writing this book, it is not known if NYCT will increase or keep the same number of questions on the next train operator exam.

Take the test under testing conditions. Clear a table or desk free of any paper and material. Have your four function calculator, watch or clock to track your time, a one-page scrap paper, pencils and this book to take the test. Power off your phone and any other electronic devices. Do not go through the other chapters of this book while taking the exam.

I strongly recommend that you do not mark your answers on the test pages. Instead, mark your answers on a sheet of paper.

Do not turn the page after completing the last question until you have completed the test. An answer key follows with detailed explanations given for each test question for further study. Even if you answer a question correctly, review the incorrect answers and its explanations. You will learn why the answer choices to a question are incorrect, and learn to think like a test writer. Test taking strategies and tips are discussed to approach the test effectively and efficiently.

Good luck and I wish you success in pursuing a career with the MTA.

TRAIN OPERATOR
EXAM NO. 1234

DO NOT OPEN THIS BOOKLET UNTIL THE SIGNAL IS GIVEN!

Write your Room Number, Seat Number and Testing Site in the spaces at the top of this page. You **MUST** FOLLOW THE INSTRUCTIONS BELOW.

ANYONE DISOBEYING ANY OF THE INSTRUCTIONS FOUND IN THE TEST INSTRUCTION BOOKLET MAY BE DISQUALIFIED AND RECEIVE A ZERO ON THE ENTIRE TEST.

FIRST SIGNAL: Follow the instructions of the test proctor.

SECOND SIGNAL: TURN TO NEXT PAGE, and begin work. This exam consists of 80 questions (1-80). Check to make sure that the test booklet goes up to and includes question number 80 and is not defective. You will have 3 hours from this signal to complete all the questions.

THIRD SIGNAL: END OF THE TEST.

Answer Questions 1-3 based on the MTA's **Winter Weather Travel Service Advisory**.

When cold or inclement weather is in the forecast, the MTA Winter Weather Travel Service Advisory is activated. During cold weather, temperatures of 10 degrees Fahrenheit or less, or freezing rain and/or ice or forecast of 5 inches of snow or more, the following changes are made:

a.   Planned service changes may be cancelled.
b.   Service on the B and W trains may end early.
c.   Express service may run local on the following lines: A, E, D, F, N, Q, 2, 3, 4,   5, 6 Express.
d.   Service on the 7 line may be reduced, with the last/first stop to/from Flushing being Times Square-42nd Street and shuttle trains providing service to/from 34th Street-Hudson Yards

During snow accumulations of 8 inches or more or freezing conditions, service on some or all routes may be reduced temporarily or suspended to clear tracks and to avoid stranding trains.

Source: www.mta.info

1. Train Operator Higgins is operating his D train under a Winter Travel Service Advisory. During the beginning of his shift, the weather forecasts that the day's temperature will be 8 degrees Fahrenheit. Throughout the day, the temperature rises by 2 degrees from 9 degrees during the morning. The temperature subsequently decreases by 3 degrees during the mid-afternoon. Snow accumulates to a high of 7 inches in the afternoon.

Which of the following may affect D train service?

A.   D train service may be reduced or suspended to clear tracks and avoid stranding trains.
B.   D express train may end early or be cancelled.
C.   A, E, B, D and Q trains will run local service.
D.   D express service may run on the local track.

2. Which of the following trains will not be affected if the Winter Weather Travel Service Advisory is activated?

A.   E
B.   6 Express
C.   R
D.   G, J and Q

3. The National Weather Service issues a Winter Advisory to the New York City area. Snow accumulates to 8 inches of snow during mid-day. By the afternoon, the temperature increases to a high of 15 degrees and snow accumulations decreases to 4 inches of snow. Which of the following is true?

A. Service on some or all routes may be reduced temporarily or suspended.
B. B and W train service may end early.
C. Train service will operate normally.
D. Planned service changes may be cancelled.

Answer questions 4-5 based on the ONE PERSON TRAIN OPERATION (OPTO) procedure.

When making a station stop under OPTO, the following procedure must be followed:

1. Bring the train to a full stop at the OPTO car stop marker in a station.
2. Place the train's brakes in full service.
3. Go to the door control position facing the correct platform. Insert the key and turn the key to the ON position.
4. Press the door opening button.
5. Make a required public address announcement.
6. Allow passengers to enter and exit the train. Doors must be fully open for at least ten seconds before closing.

4. Train Operator Chin is operating his assigned train under OPTO. He brings the train to a full stop at the OPTO car stop marker, places the brakes in full service, operates the doors by inserting the key and pressing the door opening button while facing the correct side of the platform. What is the next step that he should perform?

A.   Allow passengers to enter and exit the train
B.   Close the doors after the doors are kept open for at least ten seconds
C.   Keep the doors open for more than ten seconds if there is heavy ridership
D.   Make the required public address announcement

5. Train Operator Marcos has performed all the required OPTO procedural steps including and up to allowing passengers to enter and to exit the train. After 8 seconds, he notices that there are no additional passengers entering and exiting the train. He closes the doors and prepares for his departure from the station.

His actions are

A.   incorrect, he did not make the required public address announcement.
B.   correct, he performed the required steps for the OPTO procedure.
C.   incorrect, he did not keep the doors fully open for at least ten seconds before closing.
D.   correct, he closed the doors earlier than ten seconds since there were no additional passengers entering and exiting the train.

6. Fixed signals control the movement of a train. Fixed signals include light signals (aspects) that give a signal indication. The following are signal indications and its meanings:

(a) RED: signal indicating stop

(b) YELLOW: signal indicating proceed with caution and be prepared to stop

(c) Green: signal indicating proceed

(d) BLUE: indicates the location of an Emergency Alarm Box, Emergency Telephone and Fire Extinguisher, or an Emergency Telephone only

A train is proceeding past a light signal indicating green, and the next signal indicating yellow. What is the next MOST likely signal after the yellow aspect?

A.   green
B.   yellow
C.   red
D.   blue

7. The following sentences are prepared in an incident report involving an unauthorized person on a track and are not in order:

1-All of the passengers were escorted to the nearby platform at Beverly Road without incident.
2-The train operator encountered an unauthorized individual on the roadbed and made contact with her.
3-The Rail Control Center decided to order an evacuation of all passengers on board due to the anticipated lengthiness of the police crime scene investigation.
4-The train operator notifies the Rail Control Center that he applied his brakes in emergency upon seeing the individual on the roadbed.
5-Another train pulled up behind the out of service train to evacuate the passengers.

Which of the following order best summarizes the incident report?

A. 2,4,3,5,1
B. 2,4,5,3,1
C. 4,2,3,5,1
D. 4,2,5,1,3

8. Train Operator Diaz is operating his train at an average of 20 miles per hour. He completes the first half of his shift in 3 hours, and takes a 30-minute lunch break. He completes his remaining shift in 5 hours 30 minutes. How many miles has he travelled approximately?

A. 160
B. 170
C. 180
D. 310

9. Conductor James informs his partner, Train Operator Martinez, that he took medication before reporting to work. He explains that he is drowsy, but he is certain that he can perform his Conductor duties. They both have worked with each other for over a decade. What action should the Train Operator take?

A.   Tells the Conductor to drink a cup of coffee to ensure that he stays awake
B.   Insists that the Conductor reports his medical condition to the terminal supervisor
C.   Agrees that the Conductor will be able to perform his duties since he knows him well
D.   Ignores his medical condition since he is not a physician

10. A train yard in the Bronx holds a total of 300 subway cars. Each of the 10 storage tracks hold 3 10-car trains. The yard presently has 4 10-car trains. How many remaining train cars can be stored in the yard?

A. 230
B. 260
C. 270
D. 300

Answer Question 11 based on RESTRICTED SPEED WITH EXTREME CAUTION.

A train operator who operates at "restricted speed with extreme caution" must adhere to the following conditions:

1. Do no exceed more than ten (10) miles per hour.
2. Stop your train at least two (2) car lengths short of a visible object on the trackway.
3. Be ready to make an immediate stop.
4. Watch rails and switches for the route and observe for anything on the trackway that is unsafe to move past.
5. Be prepared to stop within one-half (1/2) your range of vision.

11. Train Operator Alvarez is operating his assigned train when he hears on his two-way radio that an unauthorized person is wandering inside a tunnel. All train operators are instructed to operate with restricted speed and extreme caution. Train Operator Alvarez reduces his speed to 12 miles per hour, watches the rails and switches for his route and observes for the individual and any obstruction on the trackway that is unsafe to move past and adheres to conditions 2, 3 and 5 above. He has performed his actions

A. correctly, he observed both the rails and switches and anything on the trackway that is unsafe to move past.
B. correctly, he observed as per the conditions above and did not need to stop his train either immediately, at least two car lengths short of an object, make an immediate stop or stop within one-half rang of his vision.
C. incorrectly, he operated his train over the maximum speed limit.
D. incorrectly, he did not sound the train horn to attempt to warn the unauthorized person.

Answer questions 12 and 13 based on Instructions for Using Fire Appliances.

Fire extinguishers are provided throughout the Transit system to protect life and property and is only used by individuals trained in the use of fire extinguishers and when they do not place themselves in a dangerous situation. Pressurized water extinguishers are used on Class A fires. Multi-purpose dry chemical (ABC) extinguishers can be used effectively on Classes A, B, and C fires. Fire extinguisher suitable for use on Class D fires must be pre-selected based on the type of metal. The following are the different classes of fires that extinguishers are to be used:

Class A: wood, paper, cloth only
Class B: flammable and combustible liquids
Class C: live electrical equipment
Class D: Combustible metals

12. A train operator while performing platform duties encounters a fire in a paper only recycling receptacle. What type of fire extinguisher would be suitable to extinguish the fire?
    A. Pressurized water extinguisher
    B. Multi-purpose dry chemical extinguisher
    C. Pre-selected fire extinguisher based on type of metal
    D. Both pressurized water and multi-purpose dry chemical extinguishers

13. A fire is smoldering inside an electrical room that powers a subway station. What is the MOST LIKELY class of fire?

    A. Class A
    B. Class B
    C. Class C
    D. Class D

Answer questions 14 and 15 based on the below information.

The Federal Communications Commission licenses The Rapid Transit Operations Radio System. The following Radio Codes are used by all operating personnel:

CODE	MEANING
A15	Fire and/or Smoke (on Train, Trackway, etc.)
B20	Flood or Serious Water Condition
C30	Derailment
D50	Request for Assistance (Police, Ambulance, etc.)
E15	Customer Under Train
F15	Serious Vandalism

14. A train operator on his two-way radio hears another train operator transmit radio codes F15 and D50. What event has occurred?

A. Serious water condition or flood
B. Derailment and a request for assistance
C. Serious vandalism and a request for police assistance
D. A customer under train and a request for assistance

15. A train operator encounters a passenger riding on top of her train. What radio code should she transmit on her two-way radio?

A. F15
B. A15
C. E15
D. D50

16. In a train operator's incident report below, the following statements are not prepared in order:

1- The train crew instructed passengers to move to the rear of the train to prepare for evacuation.
2- At approximately 1300 hours on Wednesday, January 8, 2017, a trash fire smoldered in the tunnel.
3- Power was removed and the train crew evacuated passengers on to the roadbed to Vernon Jackson Station.
4- The train operator notified Rail Control Center of a fire and smoke condition at the entering end of Hunters Point Station.
5- The Control Center notified the New York City Fire Department and ordered the evacuation of the train when power was removed.

Which of the following order of sentences best summarizes the incident report?

A. 4,1,2,5,3
B. 4,5,2,1,3
C. 2,3,1,4,5
D. 2,4,5,1,3

Answer Question 17 based on OPERATION OF LOCOMOTIVE HORN.

Whenever a locomotive has stopped for any reason, before moving again, the Train Operator must sound two long blasts of the train horn/whistle. However, every effort must be made to minimize noise in yards between 0200 to 0600 hours. During these hours, the train horn/whistle will only be sounded to alert employees on the track of train movement.

17. Train Operator Jenkins is performing his assigned duties on his midnight shift (0100 to 0900 hours) in the Jamaica train yard. During the third hour into his shift, he sounds the locomotive horn with two long blasts after a stop. Under what circumstances, would his action be correct?

A. He sounded the horn during the appropriate time between 0100 and 0900 hours.
B. He sounded the locomotive horn after his train came to a stop.
C. There were employees performing maintenance on the track to which he was operating his locomotive.
D. He sounded the locomotive horn when he saw a parked train.

Answer Questions 18-20 based on station car stop signs.

A station car stop sign indicates the positions at which a train of specific car lengths must stop. For example, a 6-car train stops adjacent to the 6-car stop marker. Each station car stop sign is located 200 feet between each sign.

Note: A station car stop sign indicating "S" is for all trains to stop at regardless of the number of subway cars.

18. A 10-car subway train is entering a station. How many feet is the train from the 10-car stop sign?

A. 200 feet
B. 300 feet
C. 400 feet
D. 600 feet

19. A subway train is adjacent to the 6-car stop sign and the train has 200 feet remaining to arrive at its station car stop sign? How many subway cars consist of this train?

A. 4
B. 6
C. 8
D. 10

20. A 4-car subway train should make a stop in the station at what car stop sign?

A. 6
B. 8
C. 10
D. S

21. Train Operators are allowed to work a maximum of 16 hours in a shift. All employees must be given an 8-hour break in between shifts before returning to work. Train Operator Kelly has completed her 16-hour shift at 10:15 AM. What time does she report for duty for her next shift?

A. 2:15 PM
B. 2:15 AM
C. 6:15 PM
D. 6:15 AM

Answer Question 22 based on the procedure for OVERRUNNING OR STOPPING SHORT OF PLATFORM.

If a train is stopped with the rear or front part of the train outside the platform, the Train Operator must do the following:

1. Signal the Conductor with one long buzzer signal not to open the doors.
2. If the train is stopped with one or more doors past the platform, the train crew notifies the Control Center.
3. The Train Operator is to assist the Conductor in allowing passengers to exit the train safely.
4. After the Train Operator returns to his/her operating position, he/she must wait for the Conductor to give two short buzzer signals before moving the train.

22. Train Operator Higgins decelerates his train, as he prepares to make a station stop. His train slides and stops outside the station platform with one door panel out. He immediately gives one long buzzer signal to his Conductor. While the Conductor is notifying the Control Center of the station overrun, Train Operator Higgins key opens the train doors to enable passengers to exit the train. He returns to his operating position. What is the next step that he must take?

A. Notifies the Control Center of the overrun incident since only the Conductor notified the Control Center.
B. Notifies the Conductor that he must inform him when he can move the train.
C. Wait for the Conductor to allow all passengers to leave the train before proceeding.
D. Wait for the Conductor to give two short buzzer signals before proceeding.

Answer Question Numbers 23 and 24 based on the below passage.

The conduct of commercial activities on any transit facility is prohibited, unless otherwise authorized. Panhandling or begging is prohibited on transit property. The conduct of certain non-transit related activities, for example, public speaking, distributing written non-commercial materials, artistic performances, including accepting donations, and solicitation for religious, charitable and political causes, are permitted.

In no event are such activities permitted on trains or buses. Employees must see that this rule is enforced and report any violation to their immediate supervisor or to a New York City Police Department Transit Bureau for enforcement.

23. A train operator witnesses a panhandler aggressively demanding money from passengers. Which of the following would be the appropriate personnel to report the incident?

 A. Conductor
B. Station Agent
C. Road Car Inspector
D. Police Officer

24. Train Operator Abrams is on the mezzanine level of a subway station. He sees a candidate running for public office greeting passengers. What is the action that he should take?
A. Promptly inform the nearest supervisor or a Transit Police Officer.
B. Inform the individual that he is not allowed to solicit political causes on transit property.
C. No action should be taken since the solicitation is not being conducted on a train or bus.
D. Greet the candidate running for public office and show your approval.

Answer Question 25 based on the policy for ARTICLES NOT TO BE CARRIED ON TRAINS OR BUSES.

Employees must not allow any individuals to carry, or convey upon, dogs or other animals unless they are secured in appropriate carriers that can be placed on the lap of a customer without interfering other customers, except that service animals and accompanying person with disabilities, or trainers carrying identifications issued by a service animal training school is permitted on trains and buses.

25.   A train operator is preparing to leave a train terminal and she sees a passenger with a dog at his side. She informs the passenger that his dog needs to be secured in an appropriate carrier. The passenger explains that he has a disability and requires the assistance of his service dog. You do not see any sign of a disability and asks that the passenger leave the train. The actions of the train operator are

A.   Correct, the train operator enforced the policy correctly in that the dog was not secured.
B.   Incorrect, the train operator did not ask for the passenger to prove his disability.
C.   Correct, the passenger did not carry identification issued by a service animal training school.
D. Incorrect, the passenger informed the train operator of a disability and he should be allowed on the train with his service dog.

26. Express trains running on a local track make only express stops unless train crews are told otherwise. However, express trains that are re-routed to local tracks due to cold weather plans, make all local station stops.

Train Operator Nieves is operating his express train and his train is rerouted over the local track from a train with mechanical problems. He is approaching a local station and the correct action that he should take is

A) skip the local station and continue to skip all stations until further instructions.
B) stop at the local station and inform passengers of the change in service.
C) to continue to make only express stops.
D) make all location station stops.

Answer Question 27 based on the procedure for TRAINS SKIPPING STATIONS.

1. Trains will enter stations being skipped at the normal speed for the area.
2. Train Operators are to decelerate gradually, and ensure that their train does not exceed fifteen (15) miles per hour while leaving the station.
3. Train Operators are required to sound a short series of blasts of the horn or whistle at the entering and leaving end of a station.
4. After the Train Operator's cab has left the leaving end of the station at fifteen (15) miles per hour, a train can resume normal speed for an area.

27. Train Operator Chen will be skipping Grand Central station. As he enters the station, he sounds a short series of blasts of the horn and decelerates gradually to fifteen (15) miles per hour. What are the next actions that he should take?

A. Ensure his train does not exceed fifteen (15) miles per hour at the leaving end of Grand Central station and resume normal speed for the area when his train operator cab is at the leaving end of the station.
B. Ensure his train does not exceed fifteen (15) miles per hour at the leaving end of Grand Central station and sound a short series of blasts of the horn at the leaving end of the station. Resume normal speed for the area when his train operator cab has left the leaving end of the station.
C. Continue his train at no more than fifteen (15) miles per hour at the leaving end of the station and sound a continuous series of blasts of the horn while skipping the station.
D. Continue his train at no more than fifteen (15) miles per hour, sound a short series of blasts of the horn at the leaving end of the station and accelerate the train gradually before the leaving end of the station.

28. The following statements are prepared in an incident report and are not in order.

1-The passengers were evacuated on to the platform at the Grand Street station.

2-While operating the southbound D train, the train's emergency brakes were activated at the entering end of Grand Street station.

3-The Train Operator investigated the cause of the brake application while the Conductor informed the Rail Control Center of the delay.

4-The Train Operator reported his findings and the Rail Control Center instructed the train crew to discharge all passengers and wait for a Train Service Supervisor.

5-After the inspection of each train car, a cause of the brakes in emergency could not be determined.

Which of the following order of statements best summarizes the incident report?

A) 2,4,1,3,5
B) 2,3,5,4,1
C) 2,3,5,1,4
D) 2,3,4,1,5

Answer Question 29 based on the Use of the Emergency Brake Valve.

The Emergency Brake valve must be activated immediately if it appears that:

- An individual is caught between the doors.
- An individual is exiting or entering between cars.
- An individual is displaying any frantic gesture.
- An individual is riding on the exterior of the train.

29. Train Operator Rahim is observing the platform as the Times Square Shuttle train leaves Grand Central. Which of the following actions would require her to activate the emergency brake valve?

A) An individual is preventing the train doors from closing.
B) An individual on the platform is gesturing frantically while the train is leaving the station.
C) An individual is riding between cars.
D) An individual is exiting from the train's doors.

30. The sentences below are contained in an incident report involving a train derailment and are not in order.

1-A reach train was routed to the location of derailment behind the disabled train to transfer the passengers.
2-The train crew observed the wheels on the lead truck on the third car and the lead set of wheels on the rear truck on the fourth car derailed.
3-A northbound C train was approaching the 81st Street Station when it derailed.
4-Once completed, the passengers were transported to 72nd Street Station where they detrained.

A. 2,1,3,4
B. 2,3,1,4
C. 3,2,1,4
D. 3,1,2,4

Answer Questions 31-35 based on the below track map of a subway yard that connects to nearby subway stations.

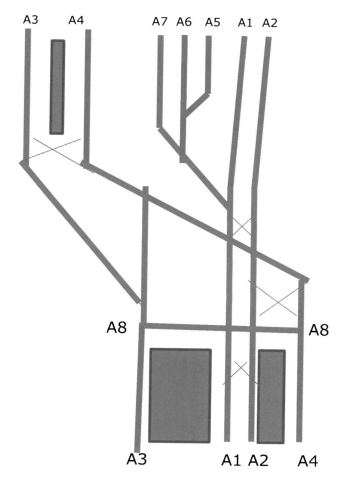

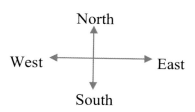

Legend:

X depicts track switches that enable trains to cross over between tracks.

[platform symbol] represents a platform that allows trains to stop and to reverse train movement in the opposite direction.

31. Which is the most efficient method for a train to operate from the northern end of track A2 to the southern end of track A3?

  A. Proceed southbound on track A2 towards the track switch on to track A1, stop at the southern end of the platform on track A1, proceed north on track A1 to the crossover track on to track A4, stop at the northern end of the platform on track A4, proceed south on track A4 towards the track switch on to track A3 and travel south on track A3 to the southern end of track A3.
  B. Proceed southbound on track A2 towards the track switch on to track A1, stop at the northern end of the platform on track A1, proceed north on track A1 to the crossover track on to track A4, stop at the southern end of the platform on track A4, proceed south on track A4 towards the track switch on to track A3 and travel south on track A3 to the southern end of track A3.
  C. Proceed northbound on track A2 towards the track switch on to track A1, stop at the southern end of the platform on track A1, proceed north on track A1 to the crossover track on to track A4, stop at the northern end of the platform on track A4, proceed south on track A4 towards the track switch on to track A3 and travel south on track A3 to the southern end of track A3.
  D. Proceed northbound on track A2 towards the track switch on to track A1, stop at the northern end of the platform on track A1, proceed north on track A1 to the crossover track on to track A4, stop at the southern end of the platform on track A4, proceed south on track A4 towards the track switch on to track A3 and travel south on track A3 to the southern end of track A3.

32. Which is the most efficient method for a train to travel from the southern end of track A3 to the platform at the southern end of track A4?

A. Proceed southbound on track A3 towards the track switch on to track A4, stop at the southern end of the platform on track A4, proceed north on track A4 to the northern end of track A4.
B. Proceed southbound on track A3 towards the track switch on to track A4, stop at the northern end of the platform on track A4, proceed south on track A4 to the southern end of track A4.
C. Proceed northbound on track A3 towards the track switch on to track A4, stop at the northern end of the platform on track A4, proceed south on track A4 to the southern end of track A4.
D. Proceed northbound on track A3 towards the track switch on to track A4, stop at the southern end of the platform on track A4, proceed north on track A4 to the northern end of track A4.

33. Which is the only track that does not travel from north to south?
    A. A4
    B. A5
    C. A7
    D. A8

34. What track allows trains to operate directly in one direction from the station located in the south to the station in the north?
A. A1
B. A2
C. A3
D. A8

35. Which is the most efficient method to operate a train from the northbound A5 track to the southern end of the platform on A2 track?

A. Proceed southbound on A5 track and merge on to A6 and A7 tracks, proceed southbound to track switch on to A2 track and proceed south on the A2 track to the southern end of the platform.
B. Proceed southbound on A5 track and merge on to A6 and A7 tracks, proceed northbound to track switch on to A2 track and proceed south on the A2 track to the southern end of the platform.
C. Proceed northbound on A5 track and merge on to A6 and A7 tracks, proceed southbound to track switch on to A2 track and proceed south on the A2 track to the southern end of the platform.
D. Proceed northbound on A5 track and merge on to A6 and A7 tracks, proceed northbound to track switch on to A2 track and proceed south on the A2 track to the southern end of the platform.

Answer Questions 36-39 about General Orders.

Before going on duty, it is the responsibility of train operators and conductors, and others whose duties involve train movement to review bulletin boards and safety notice boards for notices that affect train operations and their job duties. One such bulletin board posting is the General Order (G.O.). General Orders will be in effect until fulfilled, superseded or cancelled. Below is a General Order that is posted with service diversions.

On Mondays, Wednesdays and Fridays train service is suspended between markers 1 and 10 for routine maintenance between 2230 hours and 0500 hours. On Tuesdays and Thursdays track maintenance is performed between markers 11 and 15 from 2400 hours to 0530 hours. Weekend track maintenance work is conducted between markers 16 and 25 from Saturday at 2400 hours to Monday at 0500 hours.

During weekend track maintenance, there is no 7 train service between Queensboro Plaza and 74th Street-Broadway stations. 7 local trains run between 34th Street Hudson Yards and Queensboro Plaza stations. A shuttle bus operates between Queensboro Plaza and 74th Street-Broadway station with transfer connections at the Jackson Heights station for the E, F and R trains. The R train runs express between Jackson Heights and Forest Hills. M train service does not operate on weekends. The shuttle bus makes stops along the 7 train route between Queensboro Plaza and 74th Street-Broadway stations. A 7 train operates between 74th Street-Broadway and Flushing-Main Street that makes all local stops.

36. Track maintenance is being performed on marker 13. What day of the week and time would the G.O. be in effect?

A.   Wednesday, 0400 hours
B.   Tuesday, 0545 hours
C.   Thursday, 1200 hours
D.   Thursday, 2400 hours

37. On Fridays, what marker would not be under track maintenance?

A.   Marker 5
B.   Marker 7
C.   Marker 10
D.   Marker 25

38. A passenger asks a train operator at what station can he transfer from the 7 train to the F train to continue his trip to Forest Hills. What subway station on the 7 line is the transfer available to the F train?

A.   Queensboro Plaza
B.   Forest Hills
C.   74th Street-Broadway
D.   Jackson Heights

39. A passenger is at 34th Street Hudson Yards station and her final destination is Flushing-Main Street. Due to the weekend G.O., what is the best route for her to take?

A. Take the 7 local train from 34th Street Hudson Yards to 74th Street-Broadway. At 74th Street-Broadway, transfer to another 7 local train to continue the trip to Flushing-Main Street.

B. Take the 7 local train from 34th Street Hudson Yards to Queensboro Plaza. Transfer to a bus shuttle and continue to 74th Street-Broadway. Transfer at 74th Street-Broadway to a 7 express train to Flushing-Main Street.

C. Take the 7 local train from 34th Street Hudson Yards to Queensboro Plaza. Transfer to a bus shuttle and continue to 74th Street-Broadway. Transfer at 74th Street-Broadway to a 7 local train to Flushing-Main Street.

D. Take the 7 local train from 34th Street Hudson Yards to Queensboro Plaza. Transfer to a bus shuttle and continue to 74th Street-Broadway. Transfer at 74th Street-Broadway to a E local train to Flushing-Main Street.

40. The following sentences are contained in an incident report involving a fire and smoke condition and are not in order:

1-The Control Center notified the New York City Fire Department and Emergency Medical Service and ordered the removal of power on the tracks.
2-The uninjured passengers were issued tickets and bus service was provided.
3-The northbound E train was en route from Parson-Archer Station in Queens to World Trade Center in Manhattan, while approaching Forest Hills station.
4-The train operator reported to the Rail Control Center that the train was stopped with brakes in emergency south of Forest Hills Station in Queens, following multiple explosions and that he was experiencing a fire and smoke condition.
5-Power was removed and approximately 200 passengers on board the train were evacuated to the nearest emergency exit.

Which of the following order of sentences best summarizes the incident report?

A. 4,3,1,5,2
B. 4,3,5,1,2
C. 3,4,5,1,2
D. 3,4,1,5,2

41. A passenger runs frantically and bangs on the train operator cab window. She informs the train operator of a person on the tracks. What action should the train operator take?

A.   Descend on to the tracks to look for the person
B.   Tell the passenger to use the station customer service assistance intercom
C.   Relay the passenger's information on the two-way radio for assistance
D.   Question the passenger further to determine if the individual is truthful

Answer Question 42 based on Lost Property found in the Transit System.

Employees must send lost articles either found by them or turned over to employees by customers will be sent to the nearest location equipped with Lost Property bags. If a person finds an article on the transit system's property and refuses to give the article to an employee, the employee must inform the concerned person of the rules and procedures involving lost property. The employee, if possible, determine the name and address of the person, a description of the article, names and addresses of witnesses to the occurrence and must make a full report in writing to his/her supervisor who must immediately notify the Lost Property Office.

42. A customer informs the train operator that she has found a wallet on a bench. However, she refuses to turn over the wallet and she explains that she will contact the owner. The best course of action for the train operator is

A. Demand that the passenger turn over the wallet or the police will be summoned.
B. Agree that the customer should contact the owner of the wallet.
C. Determine the telephone numbers of the person who found the wallet and other witnesses.
D. Inform her of the rules and procedures of lost property.

Answer Questions 43-44 based on a New York City Transit Bulletin issued to its train operators.

NYCT Rapid Transit Operations (RTO) Bulletin for Red Automatic Signals

A Train Operator must STOP for a RED AUTOMATIC SIGNAL.

She/he must stop fifteen (15) feet short of the signal, or at the yellow joint marker plate on the contact rail protection board. She/he must NOT MOVE until the light turns to GREEN or YELLOW, UNLESS:

1. The signal has an "AK" sign; or
2. The signal is on a storage track or in a yard; or
3. An employee whom the Train Operator KNOWS is an authorized RTO or Electrical (Signal) employee gives a signal to go ahead which the Train Operator KNOWS is meant for him/her; or
4. The Train Operator calls the Control Center Desk Superintendent by radio and is told to proceed with RESTRICTED SPEED AND EXTREME CAUTION.

The Train Operator must call the Control Center Desk Superintendent immediately via radio. If Control Center does not acknowledge the transmission and there is no train visible ahead, he/she must wait two (2) minutes before using the wayside telephone. If after ten (10) minutes and there is a train visible ahead and Control Center still has not acknowledged the radio transmission, the Train Operator must then use the nearest wayside telephone.

43. Train Operator Diaz encounters a red automatic signal on his northbound D train with no visible train ahead. She stops her train fifteen feet short of the signal. While Train Operator Diaz's train is stopped on a non-storage track, she uses her radio to contact the Control Center Desk Superintendent. The Control Center does not acknowledge the radio transmission. What is the next action that the train operator should take?
A. Use the nearest wayside telephone if after ten minutes, there is no train visible ahead and the Control Center still has not acknowledged the radio transmission.
B. Use the nearest wayside telephone if after three minutes, there is a train visible ahead and the Control Center still has not acknowledged the radio transmission.
C. Use the nearest wayside telephone if after two minutes, there is no train visible ahead and the Control Center still has not acknowledged the radio transmission.
D. Use the nearest wayside telephone if after two minutes, there is a train visible ahead and the Control Center still has not acknowledged the radio transmission.

44. Train Operator Ruben sees an employee who is waving a lantern to proceed past a red automatic signal. He is not sure if the employee is a Rapid Transit Operations or Signal employee. He stops short ten feet from the signal and employee and confirms that the employee is from Rapid Transit Operations. Train Operator Ruben confirms that the signal to proceed past the red automatic signal is for his train. He proceeds his train past the red automatic signal. His actions are

A. Correct, he followed the appropriate steps to confirm the identity of the employee authorizing him to proceed past a red automatic signal and to confirm that the signal to proceed is meant for him.
B. Correct, he followed the appropriate steps to confirm the identity of the employee is either from RTO or Mechanical authorizing him to proceed past a red automatic signal and to confirm that the signal to proceed is meant for him.
C. Incorrect, he did not stop short fifteen feet from the red automatic signal before he confirmed the identity of the employee is either from RTO or Mechanical authorizing him to proceed past a red automatic signal and confirmed that the signal to proceed is meant for him.
D. Incorrect, he did not stop short fifteen feet from the red automatic signal before he confirmed the identity of the employee is either from RTO or Electrical authorizing him to proceed past a red automatic signal and confirmed that the signal to proceed is meant for him.

Answer Questions 45-46 based on the Brakes In Emergency Procedure.

When an undesired train's emergency brake application occurs, the Train Operator immediately notifies the Control Center. While informing the Control Center of the brakes in emergency condition, Train Operators will simultaneously attempt to recharge the air brake system. The outcome of the attempt to recharge the air brake system must be transmitted to the Control Center when it is completed.

If a train's brakes are applied in emergency due to the activation of an Emergency Brake Valve (EBV), the Train Operator investigates to determine a reason and by whom the EBV was activated. If a Train Operator is unable to obtain this information, he/she will reset the EBV, notify the Control Center, and proceed with the Control Center's approval. A Train Operator is not required to check the roadway further if it is known that an activated EBV was the cause of the emergency brake application.

If a train's brakes are applied in emergency and a Train Operator does not know why, he/she must secure the train and inspect both sides of the trackway, if possible, a sufficient distance behind the train, to attempt to determine the cause. If debris on the roadbed is the suspected cause, the Train Operator must bring a shoe paddle to remove the debris to avoid coming into contact with said debris, and to prevent the possibility of being cut by sharp objects. When leaving a train to investigate any instance of brakes in emergency, the Train Operator will make the required public address announcement, secure the train with sufficient hand brakes, on cars so equipped take along the portable radio and reverser key, and secure the cab.

45. Train Operator Michaels is leaving the Dyre Avenue station in the Bronx when his train's emergency brake application occurs. He determines that an emergency brake valve was not activated; and he is uncertain of the cause. The Control Center is notified of the brakes-in-emergency incident and he attempts to recharge the air brake system. He notifies the Control Center of the results of recharging the air brake system before he leaves the train to investigate the cause. The train and cab are secured with sufficient hand brakes applied and the cab door locked, respectively. He takes his portable radio along with his investigation. The actions of Train Operator Michaels are

A. correct, he secured the train and cab before beginning his investigation.
B. correct, he notified the Control Center, Conductor and secured his train and cab before beginning his investigation.
C. incorrect, he did not make a public address announcement to the passengers and remove the reverser key.
D. incorrect, he did not make a public address announcement to the passengers.

46. What is the next action to take after a train operator performs all the required actions before leaving his/her train to investigate brakes-in-emergency and the suspected cause is debris on the roadbed (tracks)?

A. Secure the train and cab.
B. Notify the Control Center.
C. Reset the Emergency Brake Valve.
D. Bring a shoe paddle for debris removal.

Answer Questions 47-48 based on the TRAIN HORN OR WHISTLE SIGNALS below.

NOTE: Signals prescribed below are listed "Q" for short sounds and "T" for longer sounds.

SOUND INDICATION

Apply brakes immediately (STOP): T

Sounded when passing caution lights or flags to warn personnel of the approach of a train: TT

Road Car Inspector (subway mechanic) to respond to the train: QQQ

Signal Maintainer to respond to the train: TQ

Train Crew needs (Police) Assistance: TQTQ

47. A passenger informs the Train Operator of a fight on the train. What train horn or whistle should be given?

A. TQ
B. TQTQ
C. TT
D. T

48. Train Operator Phelps sounds the QQQ horn at a terminal station. What situation below would be appropriate for this horn signal?

A. Request for a route change.
B. An immediate brake application.
C. Train's air brakes unable to charge after repeated attempts.
D. A faulty signal indicating red over red.

49. Train Operator Stamps is offered a cash reward by a passenger for finding his wallet. The passenger tells him that it's a small token of his appreciation. What action should he take?

A. Accept the tip as long as it is a small amount.
B. Accept the tip provided the passenger agrees that the amount will be split with another colleague.
C. Politely decline the tip, as Transit employees are prohibited from accepting any gratuities.
D. Encourage the passenger to donate the cash to a foundation.

Answer Question 50 based on an incident report filed by a train operator.

Location: Coney Island Yard on Track 5; Train Cab No. 68679
Observation: Inoperable public address (PA) system during a PA test.
Date and Time: November 6, 2018 at 1436 hours
Person Filing Report: Train Operator Pass No. 43487
Outcome: Requested a Car Inspector (CI) to the train for assistance.

50. Which of the following best summarizes the incident report?

A. On November 6, 2018 at 1436 hours, Train Operator pass number 43487 conducted a test of the public address system. The PA system was determined to be inoperable and a CI was requested for assistance.
B. On November 6, 2018 at 1346 hours, Train Operator pass number 43487 conducted a test of the public address system. The PA system was determined to be inoperable and a CI was requested for assistance.
C. On November 6, 2018 at 1436 hours, Train Operator pass number 43487 conducted a test of the public address system. The PA system was determined to be inoperable in Train Cab No. 68679 and a CI was requested for assistance.
D. On November 6, 2018 at 1436 hours, Train Operator pass number 43487 conducted a test of the public address system. The PA system was determined to be inoperable in Train Cab No. 68679 on track 5 in the Coney Island Yard. A CI was requested for assistance.

Answer Question 51 based on a New York City Transit Bulletin issued to its train service employees.

NYCT Rapid Transit Operations (RTO) Bulletin for Suspicious Packages

All Train Service Employees **must** be alert for suspicious bags, packages or briefcases left anywhere in the Transit system. Employees who are given with a package from an unknown individual or who encounter a suspicious item left on the tracks, platforms or trains:

- Must immediately notify the Rail Control Center (RCC)
- Must not move, open, tamper or touch a package
- Must move away from a suspicious package and separate the area
- Must wait for and follow the instructions from the NYPD and/or RCC

The following steps must be followed if a suspicious package occurs on a train:

- Proceed the train to the nearest station if a train is between stations
- When the train is properly stopped in the station, the train crew will discharge passengers and the Conductor will make a manual Public Address announcement

- If possible, advise customers of alternative routes
- Follow the instructions from the NYPD and/or the RCC

51. A train operator encounters a package on the subway tracks. All of the following are proper actions to take EXCEPT:

A. Notify the RCC immediately
B. Notify the NYPD immediately
C. Move away from a suspicious package and separate the area
D. Follow the instructions from the NYPD and/or RCC

Answer Question 52 based on the DELAY ANNOUNCEMENTS PROCEDURE.

During train delays, delay announcements **must** be given. Delay announcements must include the reason for the delay. All train service employees must remember that when a delay to train service occurs, train crews **must** keep their customers informed and avoid play pre-recorded delay announcements on cars that are equipped with the automated announcement system. The Conductor is the individual who is charged with making train announcements.   However, a Train Operator may have available information that the Conductor is not aware. In these circumstances, the Train Operator will make an announcement(s).

The first delay announcement will be made immediately. The train crew must identify themselves as the Train Operator or Conductor to the customer through the public address system, give the reason for a delay and give alternative routes. A manual announcement must be made within two (2) minutes of the first announcement and then at a minimum of every five (5) minutes if a delay is not resolved.

Public address systems may not work due to battery drain when power has been removed from the tracks and a delay has exceeded thirty (30) minutes. Train crews must confirm that their passengers are aware of the status of a delay by walking through the train and informing individuals in each car every ten (10) minutes.

52. Train Operator Jenkins is informed of a stalled train that has delayed his train. An announcement is immediately made at 2:05 PM to the passengers informing them of the delay. What are the times that the train crew is required to make a second and third announcement?

A. 2:07 PM and 2:12 PM
B. 2:07 PM and 2:10 PM
C. 2:10 PM and 2:12 PM
D. 2:05 PM and 2:07 PM

53. Train Operator Velez has worked 12 hours during his shift. Assuming that he works a maximum of 16 hours in his shift that began at 7 AM. He is given an 8-hour break in between shifts before returning to work. What time does he report to work for his next shift?

A. 7 PM
B. 7 AM
C. 3 PM
D. 3 AM

54. A R188 model subway car is approximately 51 feet in length. How many R188 subway cars in a train would fit within a 561-foot subway platform?

A. 8
B. 10
C. 11
D. 12

Answer Question 55 based on New York City Transit's SICK LEAVE POLICY.

New York City Transit's mission is to give safe, reliable and economical transportation to the public. When an employee fails to report for duty as required or abuses sick leave it affects Transit's ability to carry out its mission.

Sick Leave is appropriate when an employee is:

• unfit for work from an illness
• unfit for work from a non-service connected disability

Sick Leave is inappropriate when an employee:

• attends a routine medical/dental examination which is non-disabling
• visits a pharmacy to obtain medication
• visits an optician to obtain eyeglasses

- cares for family members who are sick
- uses sick leave for personal business

In order to be eligible for Sick Leave, an employee adhere to certain requirements:

- Employee must notify Transit of his/her intention to be absent at least one (1) hour before an employee's start of his/her shift.
- Notice must include the nature of the illness, anticipated duration of the absence and the full address and telephone number of the location where an employee can be contacted during the absence.
- During an absence, an employee must inform Transit of any changes of sick location (leaving and returning).
- For all sick absences, a Sick Leave Application must be submitted within three (3) days of return to work. If an absence exceeds two (2) days, the Sick Leave Application must include medical documentation of the illness and dates of incapacity.

55. Train Operator learns that his son will be performing at an annual school concert. However, his son's concert is on the same day that he has to work. What is the correct action that he should take?

A. Notify train supervision of his absence at least one hour before he begins his shift
B. Report to his scheduled work day since the use of sick leave is not appropriate.
C. Notify train supervision of the reason for his absence, anticipated duration of the absence and his contact information during the absence.
D. Submit a Sick Leave Application within three days of returning to work after his son's concert.

Answer Question 56 based on the DEPARTING STATIONS PROCEDURE for One Person Train Operation (OPTO)

When Train Operators who are assigned to OPTO service, a Train Operator will proceed to close the doors of his/her train when ready to depart a station and perform the following:

1. Insert door control key into key switch and turn to "ON."
2. Make required announcements alerting customers to "stand clear of the closing doors."
3. Observe platform from side window and Closed Circuit TV (CCTV) monitor where installed, operate the door closing button on the Master Door Control.
4. Observe carefully that all customers and their belongings are clear of the doors and clear of the side of the train.
5. When all side doors are closed and locked, the Master Door Control indication light illuminates.

6. Observe platform from side window and CCTV monitor where installed to again confirm that all customers and their belongings are both clear of the doors and the side of the train.

7. Turn Master Door Control Key Switch to the "RUN" position, check for the "ALL CLOSED" indication on the Master Door Control Panel remove key and return to the operating console.

8. Check CCTV monitor from the operating console that all customers and their belongings are both clear of the doors and the side of the train before moving.

9. Observe that the Train Operator's indication is illuminated and proceed to the next station stop.

56. What is the next step that an OPTO Train Operator takes after closing and locking the side doors of the train and the Master Door Control indication is lit?

A. Turn Master Door Control Key Switch to the "RUN" position, check for the "ALL CLOSED" indication on the Master Door Control Panel remove key and return to the operating console.
B. Observe that the Train Operator's indication is illuminated and proceed to the next station stop.
C. Check CCTV monitor from the operating console that all customers and their belongings are both clear of the doors and the side of the train before moving.
D. Observe platform from side window and CCTV monitor where installed to again confirm that all customers and their belongings are both clear of the doors and the side of the train.

57. A passenger accident occurs in the subways. An individual approaches a Train Operator and identifies herself as a member of the media. She questions the Train Operator of what he knows about the accident. The Train Operator should

A. explain to the reporter that an investigation of the incident is ongoing and he does not have any details.
B. inform the reporter that you cannot comment on the accident and refer her to the MTA's Media Department.
C. provide the reporter with details of the accident to the best of your knowledge.
D. verify and confirm the identity of the individual before answering her questions.

Answer Question 58 based on an incident report filed by a train operator.

Location: Canal Street station on the northbound platform
Incident: Train's brakes in emergency from a partial derailment of car number 66801
Date and Time: June 5, 2018 at 7:50 AM
Person Filing Report: Train Operator Jones

58. Which of the following best summarizes the incident report most clearly, accurately and completely?

A. Train Operator Jones reported his train's brakes in emergency on the northbound platform on June 5, 2018 at 7:50 AM.
B. On June 5, 2018 at 7:50 AM, Train Operator Jones reported his train's brakes in emergency from a partial derailment of car number 66801 on the northbound platform at Canal Street station.
C. On June 5, 2018 at 7:50 AM, Train Operator Jones reported his train's brakes in emergency from debris on the roadbed on the southbound platform at Canal Street station.
D. On June 5, 2018 at 7:50 AM, Train Operator Jones reported his train's brakes in emergency from a partial derailment on the northbound platform at Canal Street station.

59. Train Operator Chan is performing his assigned duties on his train. While the train is en route in between stations, he notices that teenagers are riding on the side of his train. What is the best course of action that he should take?

A.   Stop the train immediately and physically remove the teenagers.
B.   Apply the emergency brakes to stop the train immediately.
C.   Contact the Rail Control Center on the two-way radio for police assistance.
D.   Proceed the train to the next station at maximum speed to have the teenagers removed as soon as possible.

Answer Questions 60 based on the Bulletin issued to train operators for **Trains Striking Objects/No Brakes In Emergency.**

Train Operators are advised that any time you believe that your train has come in contact with an individual or any object along the trackway and the emergency brakes are not activated, you must comply with the following:

STOP IMMEDIATELY.

1. Call the Rail Control Center (RCC) via radio or telephone to report the incident.
2. Report the location of the incident to the RCC by giving a signal number, station name, track number or marker number.
3. Secure your train and descend to the trackway to investigate. Check for injured person(s) or possible equipment damage.
4. Report your findings to the RCC and adhere to their instructions.

60. Below are all of the correct procedures to follow when a train makes contact with an individual EXCEPT

A. Contact the FDNY immediately to request for medical assistance.
B. Contact the RCC via radio or telephone to report the incident.
C. Report the location of the incident to the RCC and give the station name.
D. Secure the train and locate the injured person.

61. Speed limits govern the maximum allowable speed for train operators to operate their trains on various sections of subway tracks. Assuming a train operator operates at the maximum speed limit for each section of the subway tracks below (in miles per hour, MPH), what is the average speed that the subway train is travelling?

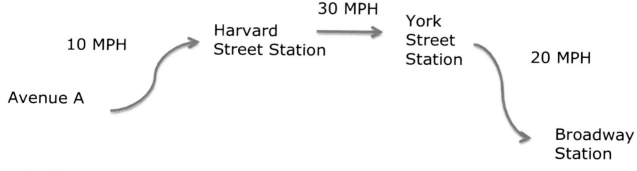

A. 15 MPH
B. 20 MPH
C. 25 MPH
D. 30 MPH

Answer Questions 62-66 based on the Bulletin issued for REPORTING UNUSUAL NOISE or CONDITION

Train crews are an important part of New York City Transit's operation safety program. Observations of unusual conditions along the tracks, if immediately report to the Rail Control Center, may prevent a serious incident.

Train crews are informed that any time you hear an unusual or loud noise or observe an unusual condition (broken rail, defects in the infrastructure, signals, car equipment or other equipment) you must following the below procedure:

1) Bring a train to a controlled stop immediately.
2) Call the Rail Control Center (RCC) via two-way radio or telephone to report the condition.
3) Report the location of the condition to the RCC by giving a survey marker number, track number, station, signal number, etc.
4) Secure your train, descend to the tracks, thoroughly inspect the tracks and underneath your train for any breaks or unusual conditions and continue inspecting the trackway for a at least a distance of 600 feet behind your train.
5) Report your findings to the RCC and follow their instructions.

Train crews are reminded that, "Employees noting defects in the signals, structure, tracks or other equipment, or any unusual conditions that would delay or make unsafe the movement of trains, must report them immediately to the RCC."

NOTE: Train Operators on trains ordered to "Stop and Stay," by the RCC MUST receive permission from the RCC before moving a train.

62. A train operator hears an unusual noise while leaving a station. He immediately brings his train to a controlled stop and smells smoke. What are the next steps that he should take?

A. Secure the train, descend to the tracks and inspect the tracks and underneath the train.
B. Call RCC and report the location of the condition.
C. Contact the RCC via two-way radio or telephone to report the condition.
D. Contact the Conductor on his train via intercom to investigate the condition.

63. Train Operator Diaz reports a defective signal and its signal number and station to the RCC. What is the required step before reporting this information to the RCC?

A. Used his two-way radio to report the defective signal condition to the RCC.
B. Secured his train to thoroughly inspect the signal and any other unusual conditions.
C. Alert his Conductor of the defective signal.
D. Report his findings from inspecting the defective signal to the RCC and wait for further instructions.

64. A Train Operator receives an order from RCC to STOP AND STAY due to a broken rail south of the 34^h Street Station on the local track. While he is waiting for further instructions, the signal displays green over yellow that enables his train to be rerouted from the local to the express track. He contacts the RCC for permission to proceed and a console dispatcher at the RCC grants his request. The actions of the train operator are

A. incorrect, he was ordered to stop and stay due to the broken rail.
B. correct, he obtained and received permission from the RCC to proceed with his train.
C. incorrect, he did not report the condition of the broken rail to the RCC.
D. correct, the signal clearly allowed him to proceed on to the express track regardless of receiving permission from the RCC.

65. Train Operator Joseph hears an unusual noise from the subway tracks while entering a subway station. He should immediately report the condition to the

A. Track Division
B. Signals Supervision
C. Rail Control Center
D. Platform Conductor

66. When an unusual condition is observed or heard, the first step a train operator should take is

A. Call the Rail Control Center via two-way radio or telephone
B. Apply the emergency brake immediately
C. Bring the train to a controlled stop immediately.
D. Identify and report the location of the unusual condition to the Rail Control Center

67. Train Operator Hayes is unclear about a directive posted on a bulletin board that was recently issued to train crews. Which of the following would be the best person to ask?

A. Another colleague who is a train operator during his break.
B. A conductor before the start of his shift.
C. A Train Service Supervisor only when the situation arises that applies to the directive.
D. A Train Service Supervisor or terminal supervisor as soon as possible.

68. Train Operator Alvarez is proceeding her train on the southbound track, and encounters a crew performing maintenance on the adjacent northbound track. She reduces her train's speed to 10 miles per hour. What is the next best course of action that she should take?

A.   Sound the horn once and proceed at the normal speed while passing the maintenance crew.
B.   Sound the horn at regular intervals while passing through the work zone.
C.   Do not sound the horn and proceed at 10 miles per hour.
D.   Proceed at the normal speed through the work zone.

Answer Question 69 based on MOVING CARS IN YARDS.

A train operator moving cars or trains in yards or on storage track must do the following:

1. Stand where he/she can see best.
2. Operate with restricted speed and extreme caution.
3. Stop at all crosswalks, stop signs and sound two (2) short blasts of the horn or whistle.
4. Observe that rails and switches are properly set.

69. Train Operator Velez is operating her train in the yard. She stands while she operates with restricted speed and extreme caution. She passes the stop signs while observing that the rails and switches are properly set. Her actions are:

A.   correct, she follow all the required actions to operate the train in the yard.
B.   incorrect, she did not follow the speed limit while operating the train.
C.   correct, she operated the train slowly and with caution.
D.   incorrect, she failed to halt at all stop signs and sound two (2) shorts blasts of the horn or whistle.

70. Train Operator Hayes is bringing his assigned train into a station. He notices a passenger leaning over the platform edge dangerously. What immediate action should he take?

A.   Apply the train's brakes immediately.
B.   Sound the horn continuously to warn the passenger.
C.   Proceed into the station without delay at the normal speed.
D.   Make an announcement that passengers should not lean over the platform.

71. Train Operator Jones is bringing her train into a station and notices two passengers on the platform engaged in a pretend fight. What action should the train operator take?

A.   Contact the Rail Control Center on the two-way radio for the police.
B.   Inform the passengers to discontinue their actions, as they could hurt themselves and other passengers.
C.   Sound the horn continuously until the passengers stop their actions.
D.   Ignore the passengers and proceed into the station.

72. A speed restriction sign is posted 600 feet before a train enters a work zone area. A train has travelled 253 feet past the speed restriction sign. What is the remaining feet before the train reaches the work zone area?

A. 347
B. 350
C. 365
D. 853

73. A train operator prepares an incident report as a result of a train collision. The following statements in the incident report are not in order:

1-A number 5 train was stopped at the home signal on Track AM at south of Fordham Road Station.

2-A number 2 train approached from the north and struck the 5 train in the rear.

3-Both trains were being transferred from Jerome Yard to 239th Street Yard when the collision occurred.

4-A collision occurred involving two 10-car trains on track AM on the number 5 line.

5-The point of collision was 300 feet south of Fordham Road station and the impact caused heavy damage both trains.

Which of the following order of sentences best summarizes the incident report?

A. 3, 5, 4, 2 and 1
B. 3, 4, 2, 5 and 1
C. 4, 1, 2, 3 and 5
D. 3, 5, 2, 4 and 1

74. Train Operator McDaniel is operating his train at an average speed of 30 miles per hour. He completes his northbound trip in 1.5 hours, and takes a lunch break for 30 minutes. He then completes his southbound trip in 2.5 hours. How many miles has he travelled?

A. 150
B. 135
C. 120
D. 102

75. Each R160 model subway train car is approximately 60 feet in length. How many R160 subway cars in a train consisting of ten cars would extend beyond the end of a 480-foot subway platform?

A. 1
B. 2
C. 3
D. 4

76. While a train is delayed and stopped at a red signal, a passenger informs the train operator that someone has stolen her wallet. Before she can respond to the passenger, the signal turns green for the train to proceed. What action should the train operator take?

A.   Inform the passenger to call the police
B.   Explain to the passenger that the train is running late, and the train operator is unable to help
C.   Inform the passenger to contact the station agent
D.   Report the stolen wallet on the two-way radio to summon the police at the next station

Answer Question 77 based on the information below.

Train Operators must apply handbrakes on at least half the cars of the train when told power will be off for 30 minutes or more, and the train being operated is in the power off area.

77. Train Operator Wong is operating his assigned train in between stations when he realizes that there is a loss of power. The Rail Control Center informs him that power will be off for at least 40 minutes. What is the minimum number of hand brakes needed to secure his 8-car train?

A.   2
B.   4
C.   6
D.   8

Answer Questions 78 based on a bulletin issued for OBSTRUCTION INCIDENTS.

An obstruction incident is defined as any incident that involves any part of a wire, cable, fixture or structure that is physically touching or has come into contact with any part of a train. When an obstruction incident occurs, the **train must not be moved** and the Train Operator must inform the Rail Control Center (RCC) immediately. The RCC will contact all relevant divisions, including the Office of System Safety (OSS) regarding an incident.

Upon supervisors' arrival, he/she must immediately contact the RCC with information of what is touching the train and any damage.

Supervision on the scene ensures that trains involved in an incident do not move until an obstruction is cleared or that the movement of trains will not affect the employee and customer safety or cause additional damage to NYCT property. Field supervision on the scene will inform the RCC when he/she has determined that it is safe to move the train.

Upon release of the equipment by OSS, the RCC will give permission for the field supervision to move the train.

78. A fixture has come into contact with the roof of a train. Under what circumstances would the train be allowed to move?

A. Permission from the Rail Control Center upon confirmation from the Train Operator that it is safe to move the train.
B. Supervisions' determination that moving the train will not affect customer and employee safety.
C. Division of Car Equipment's determination that moving the train will not affect customer and employee safety.
D. The Train Operator's determination that the fixture is cleared of any further obstruction.

79. A subway train travels 30 miles per hour and a train operator reduces her speed by 10 miles hour to clear the next signal. She further decreases her speed to 10 miles per hour as her train switches from the local to the express tracks. After her whole train clears the track switch, she resumes her train's speed of 30 miles per hour. What is the average speed that her train is traveling?

A. 20
B. 22.5
C. 30
D. 35

80. Train Operator Logan is working her PM (afternoon) shift at 1900 hours. She takes a 30-minute lunch break at 2330 hours. What time does she return to work after her lunch break?

A. 1200 hours
B. 1930 hours
C. 2330 hours
D. 2400 hours

STOP! END OF TEST

ANSWER KEY

1. D	21. C	41. C	61. B
2. C	22. D	42. D	62. B
3. C	23. D	43. C	63. A
4. D	24. C	44. D	64. B
5. C	25. D	45. C	65. C
6. C	26. C	46. D	66. C
7. A	27. B	47. B	67. D
8. B	28. B	48. C	68. B
9. B	29. B	49. C	69. D
10. B	30. C	50. D	70. A
11. C	31. A	51. B	71. B
12. D	32. C	52. A	72. A
13. C	33. D	53. B	73. C
14. C	34. C	54. C	74. C
15. D	35. A	55. B	75. B
16. D	36. D	56. D	76. D
17. C	37. D	57. B	77. B
18. D	38. C	58. B	78. B
19. C	39. C	59. C	79. B
20. D	40. D	60. A	80. D

8 TRAIN OPERATOR EXAM EXPLANATIONS

1. This question sounds overwhelming when you first read it. However, pay attention to two key pieces of information needed to answer the question. The temperature and inches of snow will help the MTA decide if and how they will implement the Winter Weather Travel Service Advisory.

First, the temperature changes throughout the day. Let's start with the initial temperature of 9 degrees. The temperature increases **by** 2 degrees, so 9 degrees+2 degrees=11 degrees. The temperature drops **by** 3 degrees, so 11 degrees-3 degrees=8 degrees.

Second, the information given in the question is the inches of snow that is 7 inches.

Let's read the question first before going to the background information needed to answer this question. The question is concerned with D train service and not any other subway line. Ignore other subway lines that are contained in the given information. We have calculated that the temperature is 8 degrees and snow has accumulated to 8 inches. The Advisory states that service changes are made when the temperature is 10 degrees or less or 5 inches of snow or more. This meets the criteria for the service changes.

Focus on one key piece of information to answer question 1, which is located in sentence C. Sentence C states that the D express service may run local. The information that states the forecast will be 8 degrees is extraneous information and irrelevant to the question. Therefore, the answer is **D.**

Incorrect Answers:

A. D train service reduced or suspended to clear tracks and avoid stranding trains would only happen if snow accumulation is 8 inches or more or if freezing conditions occurred.

B. During the activation of the Service Advisory, only the B and W trains may end early. The Advisory does not indicate the D train would end early. In fact, if the Advisory is activated, D express service may run local.

C. This is a trick answer if you are not paying attention to details. Although the A, E, D and Q express service may run local, the B is not among the lines as stated under condition C of the Advisory. Be careful of misreading an answer choice, as this is a favorite trap that test makers like to use.

TIP: The test makers like to put extra information into either a question or background information that is not relevant to answering a test item. Ignore information that is not relevant to the question and focus on specific information that helps answer a question.

2. Question 2 asks which of the subway lines contained in the answer choices will not be affected by the Service Advisory. Let's look at the choices: E, 6, R, G, J and Q subway lines. The only answer choice not listed in the Service Advisory is the R line. The answer is **C**.

Note that individuals who are familiar with the NYC subway system may know that the R line does not operate outside, but the entire route is underground. Although this knowledge is useful in answering the question correctly, it's worth the time to review the Advisory to confirm your answer.

3. This question is similar to the first question in that the Winter Advisory is activated dependent on the inches of snow and temperature. The temperature is 15 degrees and the snow accumulation is 4 inches of snow. Both the temperature and snow accumulation does not meet the conditions for the Service Advisory to be activated. Therefore, train service will operate normally. The answer is **C**.

INCORRECT ANSWERS:

A. The E train will be affected under the Advisory under condition c.

B. The 6 Express will be affected under the Advisory under condition c.

D. This is another trap answer. Although the G and J trains are not affected under the Advisory, the Q train is listed under condition c. Be careful of misreading an answer or reading part of the answer choice.

4. This type of question appears frequently throughout the Train Operator exam. NYCT gives you a set of procedural steps that are to be followed in order. A question or a series of questions will test to see if you can follow instructions. A question may give you, for example, step 3 and ask what the next step is to perform or what the previous step is to be completed before moving on to step 3.

Questions 4 and 5 deals with a train operator who is performing his duties under One Person Train Operation (OPTO). Under OPTO, Train Operator Chin has completed procedures 1-4 as described in question 4. What is the next step that Chin should follow after pressing the door opening button? Step 5 states that he makes a required public address announcement. Therefore, the answer is **D.**

INCORRECT ANSWERS:

A. Although allowing passengers to enter and to exit the train is part of the procedure, that is the not the next step to follow after opening the train doors. The train operator makes a required public address announcement after pressing the door opening button.

B. Keeping the doors open for at least ten seconds occurs after step 5; making a required public address announcement.

C. Although keeping the doors open for more than ten seconds makes sense during heavy ridership, that is not what the question is asking. Remember to follow procedures in the order given.

5. Correct vs. incorrect questions are a favorite type of question on the train operator test. The test writers are trying to assess whether you can follow policy or procedures without deviating from the standards expected of a train operator. Don't use your judgment or make up your own rules when answering the questions.

The last sentence for procedure six indicates that the doors must be fully open for at **least** ten seconds before closing. The train operator closed the doors after eight seconds, so his action is incorrect. Eliminate answer choices B and D. He must keep the door fully open for at least ten seconds. The correct answer is **C.**

INCORRECT ANSWERS:

A. Making a required public address announcement occurs after pressing the door opening button.

B. He improperly closed the doors after eight seconds. Train operators must keep the door open for **at least** ten seconds before closing.

D. This is a trick answer. Common sense would call for closing the doors earlier since there are no passengers getting on and off the train. However, this question is about assessing whether you can follow procedures or deviate from what is required of OPTO train operators. Ten seconds is the rule and train operators must follow procedures properly.

6. Before reading the signal indications and its meanings, read the question first. The question asks what the next likely signal will be after a yellow signal. Look at b under signal indications, and yellow indicates proceed with caution and be prepared to stop. A red signal would indicate stop, so the correct answer is **C.**

INCORRECT ANSWERS:

A. Green is a signal to proceed. The question is about what signal will most likely appear after a yellow signal. Green will not be a likely signal since a yellow signal indicates to a train operator to prepare to stop. A stop signal would be a red signal.

B. Individuals who have knowledge of the NYC subway signaling system would argue that two consecutive yellow signals can appear. However, we are answering the question based on the given information. The key word is MOST LIKELY. Safe train operation would entail a train operator proceeding with caution and preparing to stop in anticipation of a red signal that will follow.

D. Blue tells the location of communication devices or a fire extinguisher. The answer is incorrect.

7. Sentences that are given out of order and must be rearranged in order appears commonly on the train operator test. On most standardized tests, these types of questions are called scrambled paragraphs. Test takers should make sure that they are comfortable with answering this type of question or risk losing valuable points on the exam. Common test taking techniques involve looking for key phrases, such as but, however, similarly, etc. However, the style of these questions do not use such transitional elements. The test is concerned with the ability for test takers to understand the chronological order of events and whether they can reorder them so the facts or events make chronological sense.

The main idea of this incident is a train striking an individual on the subway tracks. What happens first? The train operator sees an individual on the roadbed and strikes her, which is sentence two (2). Immediately eliminate answers C and D. Both C and D start with sentence four (4), which is an event that occurs after the train strikes an individual when the brakes are applied in emergency.

Look at answers A and B. Both answer choices continue with sentence four (4) as the next sentence to be rearranged. Choice B is incorrect as the third sentence states that another train pulls behinds to evacuate passengers. Answer B fails to take into account that before a train pulls behind for evacuation, the Rail Control Center gives an order to evacuate passengers. Therefore, the correct answer is **A.**

8. This questions asks the approximately total number of miles that the train operator has travelled. Let's break down the calculations.

First trip is 3 hours multiplied by 20; 3*20=60 miles travelled in 3 hours.
Second trip is 5 hours 30 minutes multiplied by 20; 5.5*20=110 miles travelled in 5 hours 30 minutes.

Therefore, 60 miles+110 miles=170 miles total. The correct answer is **B.**

Note that the 30-minute lunch break does not involve any travel, so this should not be included in the calculation. If you included the 30 minute lunch break into the number of miles travelled, you would have calculated 20 miles per hour*9 hours=180 miles travelled and picked answer choice C. The test writers will give numbers that appear correct for individuals who make careless mistakes.

Note that calculators are allowed on the test.

9. Regardless of the number of years that they have worked together, operating a train while drowsy is not safe. The safe and responsible action is to report the medical condition to the terminal supervisor. The other actions would put both the train crew and passengers at risk from the train operator's drowsiness.

10. The yard holds a total of 300 subway cars. Don't get distracted by the second sentence that explains how many 10-car train sets each of the ten tracks can hold. Focus on how many train cars are in the yard and how many remaining cars can be parked in the yard. Let's calculate.

There are four (4) sets of 10-car trains; 4*10=40.
Take the difference (subtraction) between the total number of cars that this yard can accommodate and 40 cars already parked in the yard; 300-40=260 cars.

260 cars can still be stored in the yard. The answer is **B.**

11. This question is another follow the procedures and rules of NYCT. The answer choice format is correct versus incorrect and its respective reason. This is a favorite type of question that appears frequently on each train operator exam.

Skim through the question first to find out what is being asked. Compare the narrative question with the procedures. Notice that Train Operator Alvarez reduced his speed to 12 miles per hour. This is incorrect, condition one (1) states that the train cannot exceed 10 miles per hour. Therefore, his actions are incorrect because his train exceeded the maximum limit of 10 miles per hour. The correct answer is **C.**

INCORRECT ANSWERS:

A. Trick answer! The actions described in this choice are correct, but he also performed incorrectly with exceeding the 10 miles per hour speed restriction.

B. He did not need to stop his train, but he did not follow the speed limit.

D. The information given does not mention any encounter Mr. Alvarez has had with an unauthorized person on the tracks. The information states that an individual is wandering inside a tunnel. Don't misread the answer.

12. Read the question. The fire involves paper burning. Look at the different classes of extinguishers. The paragraph states that pressurized water and multi-purpose dry chemical extinguishers can be used. The correct answer is **D.**

INCORRECT ANSWERS:

A. Pressurized water extinguishers are used only on Class A fires that include wood, paper and cloth. This is correct but a multi-purpose dry chemical extinguisher may be used. This is a partially correct answer choice.

B. Again this answer is partially correct, as a pressurized water extinguisher can be used as well.

C. This is a paper fire and metals are not involved.

13. The key word is the electrical room. The only correct class of fire extinguisher to be used is Class C for live electrical equipment. The correct answer is **C.**

INCORRECT ANSWERS:

Classes A, B and D extinguisher only deal with other than live electrical equipment. The fire is in an electrical room, so only a Class C extinguisher should be used.

14. Understanding radio codes is an almost guaranteed question that appears on train operator tests. Don't memorize them as the radio code numbers and meanings can change on the test. Also the actual radio codes used in Rapid Transit Operations (RTO) are different than the codes presented on the test.

F15 is serious vandalism and D50 is request for assistance. The correct answer is **C.**

INCORRECT ANSWERS:

A. Serious water condition or flood is radio code B20.

B. Derailment is a radio code C30. D50 is a request for assistance, but the answer choice is only partially correct.

D. Radio code E15 is for a customer under a train.

15. The appropriate action for a train operator is to request for police assistance to remove the passenger. The correct answer is **D.**

INCORRECT ANSWERS:

A. F15 is applicable to serious vandalism.

B. A15 is for a fire or smoke condition.

C. E15 is for a customer under train. The train operator encounters a passenger on top of a train and **not** underneath.

16. Skim through the sentences to determine the main idea of the incident. A fire condition has occurred. The main sentence of the incident report begins with a general statement. Sentence two (2) is the appropriate introduction in the incident report. The sentence states what a train operator witnessed at the approximate time and date. Immediately eliminate answer choices A and B. Now let's look at answer choices C and D. Each choice indicates that sentences 3 and 4 should be the next sentence, respectively. Let's examine answer choices C and D.

Sentence three (3) does not make sense, as that would not be the next action to take upon discovery of a fire. You cannot remove the power and evacuate when the fire condition has not been reported without instructions from the Rail Control Center. Sentence four (4) should be the second sentence, as the train operator notifies the Rail Control Center upon discovery of the trash fire. The correct answer is **D.**

17. Specific conditions are stated that allow the use of the locomotive horn during 0200 and 0600 hours (understand and familiarize yourself with military time). 0200 hours means 2 AM and 0600 hours means 6 AM.

The third hour into Mr. Jenkins's shift is 0400 hours. The last sentence of the rule permits sounding the horn when employees on a track involving the movement of a train. Therefore, the correct answer is **C.**

INCORRECT ANSWERS:

A. Incorrect, train operators cannot sound the horn between 0100 and 0900 hours unless conditions permit such an operation of the horn.

B. Sounding the horn after coming to a stop is permitted, but the rule states between 0200 and 0600 hours, the train horn can only be used to alert employees on a track. The operator's sounding of the horn during this restricted time period is incorrect.

D. A parked train is not the condition that allows the horn to be used during the restricted time period of not using the train horn or whistle.

18. This is a series of three questions that tests your ability to calculate distance (in feet) between a train and station car stop signs. A train operator test may test your ability to calculate distances based on other signals or signs that are encountered in the

NYC subway system. Each station car stop signs tells a train operator where to stop his/her train depending on the number of subway cars that are being operated.

The diagram is the key to understanding how to calculate and to answer these questions. The distance between a subway car and the 6-car stop sign is 200 feet, and followed by an additional 200 feet each between the 8-car stop sign and the 10-car stop sign.

A 10-car train that is entering the station needs to stop at the 10-car stop sign. Multiply 200 feet and the total number of car stop signs, which is three.

Therefore, 200 feet * 3 stop signs=600 feet. The correct answer is **D**.

19. After the 6-car stop sign is the 8-car stop sign. That's a distance of 200 feet in between both signs. The question states that a subway train has 200 more feet remaining before reaching its correct station car stop sign. Therefore, an 8-car subway train will stop at the 8-car stop sign. The correct answer is **C.**

20. The answer is found in the note below the diagram. The question asks what stop sign should a 4-car train stop at. A station car stop that indicates "S" is for any number of subway cars to stop at the "S" sign. The correct answer is **D.**

INCORRECT ANSWERS:

A. A 6-car stop sign is for a 6-car subway train.

B. A 8-car stop sign is for an 8-car subway train.

C. A 10-car stop sign is for a 10-car subway train.

21. This question is asking you to calculate and to understand military time. Train operators need to determine their reporting time after completing a maximum 16-hour shift at work.

The key number is an eight (8) hour break must be given in between shifts before returning to work. Let's do some addition.

10:15 AM + 8 hours later = 1815 hours (or 6:15 PM). After Ms. Kelly's eight hour break, she will need to report to her next shift at 6:15 PM. The correct answer is **C.**

Answer choice D is a trap answer if you are not paying attention to whether the time to report to work is AM or PM. Answer choices A and B are incorrect and designed for individuals who misread and miscalculate the the time by adding 16 hours instead of 8 hours.

Reference Table:

MILITARY TIME TRANSLATION:

0100 hours	1 AM
0200 hours	2 AM
0300 hours	3 AM
0400 hours	4 AM
0500 hours	5 AM
0600 hours	6 AM
0700 hours	7 AM
0800 hours	8 AM
0900 hours	9 AM
1000 hours	10 AM
1100 hours	11 AM
1200 hours	12 PM
1300 hours	1 PM
1400 hours	2 PM
1500 hours	3 PM
1600 hours	4 PM
1700 hours	5 PM
1800 hours	6 PM
1900 hours	7 PM
2000 hours	8 PM
2100 hours	9 PM
2200 hours	10 PM
2300 hours	11 PM
2400 hours	12 PM (midnight)

22. This is another procedures question and if you can follow the rules as a train operator. Read the question first before reviewing the procedures to take during a platform overrun. You are being asked what is the next step to take after the train operator returns to the train cab. The answer is in the fourth step. A train operator is to wait for two short buzzer signals from the Conductor before train movement. The correct answer is **D.**

INCORRECT ANSWERS:

A. His conductor has already notified the Control Center, and the train operator does not need to repeat the information again about the station overrun.

B. Incorrect, the train operator waits for two short buzzer signals before he can move the train.

C. The passengers have already been allowed to exit before the train operator returned to his operation position.

23. Questions based on transit directives or memos issued to employees are frequently tested. Always read the question first to know what to look for in the directives or memos.

Panhandling of any kind whether aggressive or passive is not allowed on Transit property. The last sentence directs employees to report a violation to their immediate supervisor or Transit Police. A Police Officer would be the appropriate individual for enforcement. The correct answer is **D.**

The titles of Conductor, Station Agent and Road Car Inspector are neither a train operator's immediate supervisor or member of the Transit Police.

24. Political causes are allowed on Transit property, as long as the activities aren't on trains or buses. The information given in the question states that the candidate is conducting his/her cause in a subway station. He is not conducting political causes on a train or bus, so this is allowed and no action should be taken. The correct answer is **C.**

INCORRECT ANSWERS:

A. Political causes are allowed on transit property except on subways and buses. The candidate is inside a subway station, and is not violating any rules.

B. Political causes qualify under non-transit related activities that are allowed.

D. Public employees should not engage in political activities while on duty and in their performance of their job duties.

25. Another correct vs. incorrect type of question. Service animals are allowed on trains and buses. It is not appropriate for an employee to determine if there are any visible signs of a disability. The passenger informed a train operator of a disability and a need for his service dog. Therefore, he should be allowed on the train. The correct answer is **D.**

INCORRECT ANSWERS:

A. The passenger has informed the train operator of a disability and the use of a service dog. This is an exception to the policy stating that service animals do not need to be secured in appropriate carriers.

B. The policy does not require that passengers submit evidence of a disability. This is also a violate of an individual's privacy.

C. Identification is only required for trainers from a service animal training school.

26. Read the question first before skimming through the information given. Mr. Nieves's express train is being rerouted on to a local track. The first sentence in the information given before the question is that express trains on a local track make express stop unless told to make local stops. Since he has not been told to make local station stops, he will continue to stop his express train at express stops. The correct answer is **C.**

INCORRECT ANSWERS:

27. A procedures based question. The last sentence in the question states that Train Operator Chen's train has decelerated to 15 miles per hour. What should he do next? Let's look at the procedures and zero in on the next steps that must be taken. Steps 3 and 4 give the answer to this question. Maintain the train's speed at no more than 15 miles per hour, sound a short series of blasts of the horn when entering and leaving Grand Central station and resume normal speed after his train operator cab passes the leaving end of Grand Central station.

The correct answer is **B.**

INCORRECT ANSWERS:

A. The actions performed are correct, but the train operator did not sound a short series of blasts of the horn or whistle when entering and leaving Grand Central.

C. Continuous blasts of the horn is incorrect. A train operator is required to sound a **short** series of blasts of the horn or whistle.

D. Accelerating the train gradually before leaving the station is a violation of. He can only resume normal speed for the area **after** his train operator cab has left the leaving end of a station.

28. Another scrambled paragraph question that asks you to rearrange the sentences in order for an incident report. Determining the main sentence for the incident report is not necessary since all answer choices begin with sentence 2.

Let's examine the sentences. A D train's emergency brakes were activated. The next event would be to have a train crew member inform the Rail Control Center of the emergency brake incident and for the Train Operator to investigate the cause. This would be sentence number three (3). So answer choice A is eliminated since sentence four (4) would not be the next event of the RCC ordering the discharge of all passengers.

Let's look at the next event that occurs after the train operator goes to investigate the incident. Sentence five (5) details the findings of the train operator's investigation in that a cause could not be determined. So far the order of sentences is 2, 3 and 5. We eliminate answer choice D since there is no explanation of what happened between the inspection of the train and the evacuation of the passengers.

We are left with answer choices B and C. Between the remaining sentences of one (1) and four (4), sentence four is the most appropriate event to occur next as after the investigation of the brake application. The Train Operator notifies the outcome of his investigation to the RCC and discharge instructions are given **before** the passengers are evacuate on to the platform. The correct answer is **B.**

29. This question gives scenarios of when an emergency brake valve should be applied. After reviewing the question, look at the conditions that permit the use of the emergency brake valve. Now look at the answer choices that apply to the conditions. Choice B states that an individual is displaying a frantic gesture while the train is leaving. The third conditions states an individual displaying any frantic gesture calls for the emergency brake valve to be activated. The correct answer is B.

INCORRECT ANSWERS:

A. Answer choice A is incorrect since the individual is hold the doors open and not that he/she is caught between the doors.

C. This answer choice states a passenger is riding between the cars. Based on the conditions given, the brake valve is only applied if an individual is exiting or entering between the train cars. So this answer is incorrect.

D. Choice D is incorrect. A passenger is leaving from the train's doors which is not an emergency situation. Should a passenger exit between a train's cars, the train crew would apply the emergency brakes.

30. The test makers sure like their scrambled paragraph questions. The opening sentence of the incident report starts with either sentence two (2) or three (3). Sentence two is not an appropriate introduction to the report since details of a derailment is given. What occurred before the derailment? Eliminate answer choices A and B. We have choices C and D remaining.

The second sentence that should be in the incident report is either sentence two (2) in answer choice C or sentence one (1) in answer choice D. Sentence 1 is a conclusion of what action was taken as a result of the derailment with a reach train to transfer the passengers. Sentence 2 details the train crew's findings from investigate their train derailment. Therefore, the correct answer is **C.**

31. A visual map or diagram will very likely appear on any train operator test. Study the diagram and get a general understanding of what information is being given. Sometime a visual aid will be accompanied by a long reading passage. My test taking experience shows that a visual is more likely to help you answer the test question quicker than reading the text.

These series of questions ask you what is the most efficient or most direct way to go from one location to another location. Start by reviewing the question and eliminate the answer choices that do not make sense. The question asks how a train can go from the northern end of track A2. Since you are the northern end of a track already, how can you continue going northbound? Eliminate answer choices C and D. Now review answer choices A and B while following the information with the track map given.

Start with answer choice A. A train starts at the northern end of track A2. You are at the end of the track, so your train can only proceed southbound. You can immediately eliminate answer choices C and D since they indicate a train proceeds northbound.

The legend indicates an X means a train can switch from one track to another track. The southbound train crosses over on a track switch to track A1, which is consistent with the map given. Once the train is on track A1, the train makes a stop at a platform on the southern end of track A1. The legend indicates that a platform allows trains to stop and move in the opposite direction. So far this answer choice is correct. Let's continue reading. After stopping at a platform, a train operator moves the trains northbound on track A1 that allows him to crossover to track A4 going to the northern end of this track. The train is allowed to stop at a platform adjacent to track A4 and go in the opposite direction. The train moves south on track A4 after leaving a platform and crosses over on a track switch on to track A3. The train travel south on track A3 and allows the train to arrive at its intended destination at the southern end of track A3. The correct answer is **A.**

Answer choice B is incorrect since the platform on track A1 is located on the southern end of the track. If you look at the map, there is no platform north on track A1.

32. Another questions that calls for you to review the most efficient method for a train to get to its destination. Instead of reading the answer choices, let's look at the question. The train is already at the southern end of track A3, which means that you cannot continue to go further south. Answer choices A and B don't make sense since the answer states that a train proceeds southbound. This saves us time in reviewing the remaining answer choices C and D.

Follow the map while reading answer choice C. A train is at the southern end of track A3, so the train proceeds north on track A3. Since the train needs to be on track A4, the train needs to travel across a track switch on to track A4. The platform at the northern end of track A4 allows the train to make a stop before a train operator moves the train in the opposite direction to the southern end of track A4 (our destination). The correct answer is **C**.

Answer choice D makes no sense since the question is asking how a train can terminate at the southern end of Track A4. This answer choice indicates that a train stops at the northern end of track A4.

33. Looking at the compass given in the track map and reviewing the track designations, the only track that does not travel north to south is track A8. Track A8 travel west to east and vice-versa. The correct answer is **D**.

Tracks A4, A5 and A7 all travel north to south (looking at the track map), so these answer choices are incorrect.

34. The question is what track allows a train to go directly from a station located in the north to a station in the south. Answer choices A1, A2 and A8 can be immediately ruled out since tracks A1 And A2 have no platforms in the north and track A8 has no stations at all. Track A3 has a platform on the northern end of its track. The correct answer is **C.**

35. Since the question gives information that a train is on the northbound track, you can immediately eliminate answer choices C and D. Let's read answer choice A. Looking at the track map given, a train can move south on track A5 and and merge on to track A6 and finally merge on to track A7. Upon a train moving south on track A7, the track is joined with track A1 with a track switch to track A2 (our destination track). The track switch enables a train to continue south on track A2 and terminating at a platform that is adjacent to the southern end of track A2, which is our final stop.

For answer choice B, proceeding northbound is incorrect since according to the track map, the track switch is located south after merging on to track A1.

36. Always take note of the heading that informs you what questions are relevant to information given on the test. In this case, questions 36 to 39 concern the reading passage about General Orders.

Read the question first before identifying the information in the reading passage for the answer. Maintenance is being done on marker 13. Let's look at the reading passage where it states when maintenance occurs on marker 13. The sentence states, "On Tuesdays and Thursdays track maintenance is performed between markers 11 and 15 from 2400 hours to 0530 hours." Answer choice A can be immediately eliminated since no maintenance is done on Wednesdays for marker 13.

Both answer choices B and C are incorrect since 0545 hours and 1200 hours are times when maintenance is not occurring. Let's examine answer choice D in that Thursday at 2400 hours is a time when the maintenance begins for marker 13. The correct answer is **D.**

37. On Fridays, only markers 1 through 10 are under maintenance. Markers 5, 7 and 10 all fall under the Friday maintenance schedule so answer choices A, B and C are incorrect. Marker 25 is outside of this range of markers under maintenance on Fridays. The correct answer is **D.**

38. The 74th Street on the 7 line allows transfer connections at Jackson Heights station to the F line. The station to transfer is 74th Street-Broadway. The correct answer is **C.**

INCORRECT ANSWERS:

A. Queensboro Plaza has no F train service.

B. Forest Hills is the station that a passenger wants to travel to. Be careful of misreading the question.

D. Jackson Heights is the station for the E, F and R trains and not the station name on the 7 line. Trick answer!

39. The G.O. is headache for this passenger. The last paragraph gives the information needed for her to travel from the Hudson Yards to Main Street stations. 7 train service is available from Hudson Yards to Queensboro Plaza. A shuttle bus replaces no train service from Queensboro Plaza to 74th Street-Broadway stations. She will need to take a shuttle bus when her 7 train terminates at Queensboro Plaza and continue her trip to 74th Street. At 74th Street, she can continue on to Flushing-Main Street by taking a 7 train that operates between 74th Street and Main Street stations. Review the answer choices and the correct answer is **C.**

40. A scrambled paragraph question. Look at the answer choices and either the first sentence begins with sentence three (3) or four (4). Sentence 3 gives information of the direction of the E train that it was travelling with the key words that the train was approaching Forest Hills. Sentence 4 states the incident that occurred. Sentence 3 is the opening statement written in the incident report. Immediately eliminate answer choices A and B. Both choices C and D agree that sentence 4 is the next best sentence. What differs is whether sentence 5 or sentence 1 should be the next sentence. Review both statements and determine whether sentence 5 or 1 should be after sentence 4.

In sentence 4, the train operator reported the situation to the Rail Control Center. Sentence 1 states the Control Center notifies the Fire Department and Emergency Medical Service once this information was relayed, and ordered power removal. Sentence 5 states that power was removed and passengers evacuated. Sentence 1 should then precede sentence 5 given the sequence of the events. The correct answer is **D.**

41. This is a judgment question that a train operator should take under an emergency and stressful situation. Remember that passenger safety is of the utmost importance in this job.

Action must be taken immediately to protect the safety of an individual on the tracks. The best answer choice is to use a train operator's radio to notify the incident for follow up assistance to protect this individual from harm. The correct answer is **C**.

INCORRECT ANSWERS:

A. Descending on to the tracks will compromise you and the other individual's safety when trains are operating in the area.

B. It's a transit employee's responsibility to take action when a passenger has notified you of an incident. Asking a passenger to report it to customer service when you have been notified as a Transit employee is neglecting your duties.

D. The train operator's responsibility is not to question the truthfulness of a passenger who has informed you of an emergency situation. A train operator should take the necessary action to protect the safety of passengers.

42. According to the information given, "If a person finds an article on the transit system's property and refuses to give the article to an employee, the employee must inform the concerned person of the rules and procedures involving lost property." Therefore, the train operator should inform the passenger what the rules and procedures are required for lost property. The correct answer is **D**.

The other answer choices do not address the issue of the passenger who refuses to turn in the lost property. They are violations of what is required by the directive issued to employees.

43. Read the question first before reviewing the Transit bulletin. The train operator has radioed the Control Center without acknowledgement. The last paragraph indicates that a train operator must wait two minutes before using a telephone. No train is visibly ahead, so after two minutes, Ms. Diaz can use a nearby telephone to contact the Control Center. The correct answer is **C**.

INCORRECT ANSWERS:

A. A train operator is allowed to use a wayside telephone after two minutes **not** ten minutes provided that there no train ahead and the Control Center has not acknowledged the radio transmission.

B. A train operator is allowed to use a wayside telephone after two minutes **not** ten minutes provided that there no train ahead and the Control Center has not acknowledged the radio transmission..

D. If you picked this answer, you might have misread that this choice indicates that a train is visible ahead. Train operators use a telephone after two minutes when a train is **not** visible ahead.

44. Train Operator Ruben performs all of the required actions **except** for stopping short ten (10) feet from a signal and employee. The bulletin states **15 feet**. Any answer choices that state correct can be immediately eliminated, which are choices A and B.

Both C and D sound correct, but if you read the choices carefully, answer choice C states Mechanical employee. The bulletin states **Electrical (Signal)** employee. The correct answer is **D.**

45. The last sentence in the last paragraph of the information given has the answer to this question.

Although the train operator secured the train cab, applied sufficient hand brakes and took his portable radio for the investigation, he did not perform two required actions. He did not make a public address announcement and take his reverser key. The correct answer is **C.**

INCORRECT ANSWERS:

A. Securing the train and cab are not the only required actions that he must perform before beginning his investigation. He did not make an announcement to passengers and he did not remove his reverser key.

B. The train operator did not fulfill all of the required actions before launching his investigation. Pay attention to the list of actions that he performed and compare them to the information given. If he has only complete part of the required steps, his actions are overall, incorrect.

D. This is not the only incorrect action that he performed. He did not remove his reverser key.

46. In the last paragraph, a sentence states, "If debris on the roadbed is the suspected cause, the Train Operator **must bring a shoe paddle to remove the debris** to avoid coming into contact with said debris, and to prevent the possibility of being cut by sharp objects." The correct answer is **D.**

The other actions listed in answer choices A, B and C are not relevant since the question has stated that the train operator has performed all of the required actions before leaving his train to investigate. The key information is that the train operator suspects the cause of the emergency brakes is from debris.

47. Train horn or whistle signals have consistently appears on past train operator tests. The key is not to memorize the signals, but to understand how to apply the signals to a situation appropriately.

A fight on a train would require police assistance. Reviewing the information given, TQTQ would be the correct signal to summon the police. The correct answer is **B.**

INCORRECT ANSWERS:

A. TQ is used to summon a signal maintainer.

C. TT is the signal used for passing caution lights or flags to warn of an approaching train.

D. T is used to apply the brakes immediately.

48. QQQ represents summoning a road car inspector to a train. Let's review the answer choices that would most likely be the appropriate signal.

Answer choice A is a request for a route change. A subway mechanic would not be needed.

Answer choice B is for an immediate brake application. This would be a T signal.

Answer choice C is for an ability to charge the train's air brakes. A subway mechanic would be the most appropriate personnel for this situation. The correct answer is **C.**

Answer choice D would be appropriate for a signal maintainer to respond with a TQ signal.

49. This is an ethics and employee conduct question. Government employees should not accept any monies or have an appearance of a conflict of interest at all times. The appropriate response is to politely decline the cash. The correct answer is **C.**

50. This type of question asks you to best summarize a number of facts or observations provided. This question type appears less frequently than scrambled paragraphs. However, it's important to acclimate yourself to answer these questions correctly.

The sequence of events that occur is a key important strategy to answer this question correctly. The questions asks for the best summary for an incident report as opposed to reordering sentences.

Answer B is incorrect as the time of 1346 hours is incorrect.

The sequence of events are that a train operator was testing the public address system and determined that it was not operable. The outcome was to request a car inspector for assistance. Now let's look at the remaining answer choices A, C and D.

Choice A is incorrect, as the summary fails to state where the public address system is inoperable. It is in cab number 68679.

Choice C does not state what track the train is located on that has an inoperable PA system.

The correct answer is **D.** The summary gives the complete information of the date and time, the employee's pass number who conducted the PA test, the cab number that has the inoperable PA system, the track number and name of the yard and a request for a car inspector.

51. Notifying the RCC, moving away from suspicious packages, separate the area from a package and following the NYPD and/or RCC instructions are the correct actions outlined in the bulletin. However, notifying the NYPD is not outlined in the bulletin and is the only improper action among the answer choices. The correct answer is **B.**

52. The procedure requires a second announcement made two (2) minutes after the first announcement and at least every five (5) minutes if a delay is not resolved.

Two minutes after the first immediate announcement at 2:05 PM would be 2:07 PM and a subsequent five minute announcement would be at 2:12 PM. The correct answer is **A.**

53. The twelve hours that Mr. Velez has worked is irrelevant to answering the question. He works a 16-hour shift starting at 7 AM. 0700 hours+16 hours=2300 hours or 11 PM. An eight (8) hour break would mean that he returns at 7 AM for his next shift. 2300 hours+8 hours=0700 hours or 7 AM. The correct answer is **B.**

54. If a subway platform is 561 feet long and each subway car is 51 feet in length, we would divide the length of one subway car (in feet) from the total feet of a subway platform to determine how many subway cars would fit. Therefore,

561 feet (platform length)/51 feet (each subway car length)=11 subway cars.

The correct answer is **C.**

55. The situation given in this question is that a train operator is scheduled for work, but he wants to attend his son's concert. This would make the train operator ineligible for sick leave based on the examples given of when sick leave is inappropriate. Note the bullet point states using sick leave for personal business is inappropriate. Answer choices A, C and D make him ineligible since he already cannot use sick leave.

The train operator is expected to report to work as scheduled. The correct answer is **B.**

56. A laundry list of procedures or steps to follow appears throughout a train operator exam. Rather than read through all of the procedures, read the question first to determine what information should be identified to answer a question.

The question asks what the next step should be after closing and locking the side train doors, and the Master Door Control indication is lit. The answer is step six (6). Observer the platform from the window and CCTV monitor to confirm clearance of customers and their belongings from the train. The correct answer is **D**.

INCORRECT ANSWERS:

A. This is step seven and is completed after a train operator observers and confirms all customers are cleared from the train after closing the doors.

B. This is the last step to take once steps one through eight are completed.

C. This is the second to last step to complete and is **not** the next step to follow after closing and locking the train doors.

57. Transit employees should never make pubic statements to the media. All inquiries from the media should be addressed to the MTA's media department. The correct answer is **B**.

58. When answering questions that involve summarizing various facts, ensure the facts are correct, complete and in sequence of events that occurred.

We are given the facts that on June 5, 2018 at 7:50 AM, a partial train derailment occurred involving a train car on the northbound platform at Canal Street station.

Let's review the answer choices. We can immediately eliminate answer choice C since the facts are incorrect. The brakes in emergency was not from debris on the roadbed and the incident didn't happen on the southbound platform.

Answer choice A contains incomplete information without the reason for the emergency brakes to be activated and location of the incident.

Answer choice B contains the date, time, name of train operator involved, the emergency brake application and the cause and location of the train car number and the location and name of the subway station. The correct answer is **B**.

Answer choice D does not give the location of the train derailment (ie. Train car number).

59. This is a judgment question in ensuring the safety of customers on transit property.

Let's review the choices.

Choice A involves unnecessary physical contact with passengers. This is not the responsibility of a train operator.

Choice B is a dangerous action that can hurt the teenagers by applying the emergency brakes.

Choice C that involves communicating a train operator's observation and requesting police assistance is the responsible and safe action to take.

Choice D involves operating the train at maximum speed which may compromise the safety of the teenagers riding outside the subway car. This would be an unsafe and irresponsible action.

60. Answer choices B, C and D are all listed in the Bulletin of the actions to comply with when making contact with an individual. Contacting the FDNY is not part of the protocol to follow. The correct answer is **A.**

61. The question asks you to assume a train is operating at the maximum speed for each section of the track. You are being asked what is the average speed that this subway train is travelling. The word average means the following:

1) Add all the numbers (sum)
2) Divide by how many numbers there are (count)

Formula:

$$\frac{Sum}{Count}$$

Calculate as follows:

$$\frac{10+30+20}{3} = 20$$

Therefore, the average speed that this train has travelled is 20 miles per hour. The correct answer is **B.**

62. Most of the bulletins and reading passages have limited information that is relevant to answer test questions. Questions 62-66 rely on a lot more information from the bulletin.

After stopping his train, steps 2 and 3 require calling the RCC and reporting the location of the condition. The correct answer is **B.**

Both answer choices A and D are incorrect. Choice A is the fourth step to take **after** contacting the RCC and reporting a condition. The bulletin does not mention contacting the Conductor to investigate contained in answer choice D.

63. This question is asking you what is the previous step to complete before reporting the location of a defective signal. The answer is to contact RCC and report a defective signal. The correct answer is **A.**

INCORRECT ANSWERS:

B. Securing the train to inspect the signal is done after reporting the location of the condition to RCC.

C. The bulletin does not mention anywhere to alert the Conductor.

D. Reporting findings is the last step to complete in the procedure. This would not be the previous step before reporting a defective signal.

64. The answer is found in the note section of the bulletin.

NOTE: Train Operators on trains ordered to "Stop and Stay," by the RCC MUST receive permission from the RCC before moving a train.

Even though the signal enabled him to proceed on to a rerouted track, the train operator correctly obtained and received RCC's permission to move his train. The correct answer is **B.**

INCORRECT ANSWERS:

A. Although it is correct that he received a stop and stay order, the train operator did obtain approval to proceed on to a rerouted track.

C. The broken rail was already reported to the RCC to a stop and stay order was issued to train operators.

D. This answer is incorrect if the train proceeded without obtaining and receiving RCC's permission. Train operators must receive permission from the RCC before moving a train.

65. The bulletin clearly states that the Rail Control Center must be immediately notified. The track and signals department and platform conductor are not the personnel to notify when reporting a condition. The correct answer is **C.**

66. The first step outlined in the Bulletin is to bring the train to a controlled stop immediately. The correct answer is **C.**

Contacting the Rail Control Center and reporting the location of an unusual condition for answer choices A and D, respectively, are steps taken later.

Applying the emergency brake immediately is against policy in answer choice B. The correct action is to bring a train to a controlled stop.

67. This is a judgment question for train operators to exercise a safe and responsible action. The best action is to ask a member from supervision to clarify a directive. Asking other non-supervisors may be beneficial, but supervision is the authority on interpreting and implementing Transit directives to train crews. Waiting for a situation to arise, as related to a direct, before asking is irresponsible and compromise the safety of the train operator and others. The correct answer is **D.**

68. Sounding the horn regularly ensures the safety of maintenance crew performing work around the moving train. The correct answer is **B.**

INCORRECT ANSWERS:

A. Proceeding at the normal speed jeopardizes the safety of the maintenance crew around the train. Maintaining a slower speed reduces the likelihood of accidents.

C. Failing to sound the train horn to warn maintenance personnel of an approaching train is unsafe and endangers employees.

D. Proceeding at the normal speed in a work zone area is unsafe and irresponsible.

69. The third item requires train operators to stop at all crosswalks and stop signs. Ms. Velez failed to come to a complete stop at all stop signs. Eliminate answer choices A and C. Answer choice B is incorrect since she operated at restricted speed and extreme caution.

Ms. Velez's incorrect actions are failing to halt at all stop signs and failing to sound two short blasts of the horn or whistle. The correct answer is **D.**

70. The safety of passengers is an important job function of train operators. To avoid probable injury, applying the brakes protects the passenger acting unsafely. The correct answer is **A.**

INCORRECT ANSWERS:

B. Sounding the horn continuously may alarm the passenger and is counterproductive to end a dangerous situation of the passenger leaning over the platform edge.

C. Proceeding into the station without delay increases the risk of injury the passenger and making contact with him/her.

D. Making an announcement as opposed to stopping the train immediately does not resolve an immediate danger that the passenger is facing.

71. The most direct solution to avoiding passenger injury and enhancing the safety of others around them is to ask them to stop their pretend fight. The correct answer is **B.**

The other answer choices do not resolve an immediate danger of the passengers hurting themselves or those around them on the platform. A pretend fight does not warrant police intervention as listed in answer choice A.

72. A speed restriction sign is posted 600 feet before a work zone area. The train operator needs to determine how many feet remaining (subtraction) until the train reaches the work zone area. Since the train has proceeded 253 feet past the sign, we will need to subtract the difference between 600 feet and 253 feet.

600-253=347 feet before reaching the work zone.

The correct answer is **A.**

73. We have a choice between sentences three (3) or four (4) as our opening statement in the incident report. Statement 3 is concerned with why both trains were on the same track at the time of the collision. Statement 4 states that a collision had occurred involving two trains with the location of the track and train line. Statement 4 would be the appropriate introduction. The correct answer is **C.**

74. To calculate the number of miles travelled, we need to multiply the total hours spent on the train operator's total trips, which is 1.5 hours+2.5 hours, or a total of 4 hours, with the average speed of 30 miles per hour.

4 hours*30 miles per hour=120 miles travelled

The correct answer is **C.**

75. Take the difference between the total feet of a 10-car train and the 480 feet platform to determine how many subway cars extend beyond the platform.

Since each train car is 60 feet, multiply by 10 subway cars, which is 600 feet.

The difference is 600 feet-480 feet (platform)=120 feet.

The 10-car subway train has extended 120 feet past the platform. Since each subway car is 60 feet in length, 120 feet means that two subway cars have extended beyond the platform. Or 120/60=2 cars. The correct answer is **B**.

76. Regardless of the train delay and the proceed signal, the train operator has been notified of a crime that has occurred. The train operator must report the incident and summon for police assistance. The correct answer is **D**.

The other actions shirk the responsibilities of employees who have been notified of an incident and an appropriate response and action must be followed up.

77. Since power will be off for over 30 minutes, handbrakes are required on at least half of the train cars. Since the train has 8 cars, at least 4 train cars need to have hand brakes. ½ of 8 train cars=4. The correct answer is **B**.

78. The third paragraph states that supervision will allow the movement of trains if it doesn't affect employee and customer safety. The correct answer is **B**.

INCORRECT ANSWERS:

A. Movement of a train after contact with a fixture is not granted by the Rail Control Center. Supervision on the scene has the authority to determine if a train can be moved.

C. Division of Car Equipment is not involved with train movement after contact is made with an object.

D. The train operator does not have authority to determine if a train can be moved even if a fixture is no longer in contact with a train. Only supervision on the scene can make that decision.

79. This is an average speed calculation question. Below is a summary breakdown of the numbers to calculate.

30 mph
20 mph (reduction of speed **by** 10 mph to clear next signal)
10 mph (further reduction of speed **to** 10 mph)
<u>30 mph</u> (resuming speed of 30 mph after clearing track switch)
90 mph (total)

Let's calculate.

90/4 (numbers in the set)=22.5 mph (average speed)

The correct answer is **B.**

80. The 1900 hours given in the question is irrelevant to calculating what time Ms. Logan should return from her lunch break.

2330 hours+30 minutes=2400 hours or 12 AM. The correct answer is **D.**

Be careful of answer choice A, as 1200 hours means 12 PM and not 12 AM. Refer to the military time table for further reference and study on page eighty-six (86).

9 CONDUCTOR EXAM

This chapter contains multiple choice questions that are specifically for the Conductor exam. Be sure to complete the test questions in Chapter 7 since most of the content for both the train operator and conductor exams overlap.

Take the test under testing conditions. Clear a table or desk free of any paper and material. Have your four function calculator, watch or clock to track your time, a one-page scrap paper, pencils and this book to take the test. Power off your phone and any other electronic devices. Do not go through the other chapters of this book while taking the exam.

I strongly recommend that you do not mark your answers or make any notes on the test pages. Instead, mark your answers on a sheet of paper.

Do not turn the page after completing the last question until you have completed the test. An answer key follows with detailed explanations given for each test question for further study. Even if you answer a question correctly, review the incorrect answers and its explanations. You will learn why the answer choices to a question are incorrect, and learn to think like a test writer. Test taking strategies and tips are discussed to approach the test effectively and efficiently.

Good luck and I wish you success in pursuing a career with the MTA.

CONDUCTOR
EXAM NO. 1234

DO NOT OPEN THIS BOOKLET UNTIL THE SIGNAL IS GIVEN!

Write your Room Number, Seat Number and Testing Site in the spaces at the top of this page. You **MUST** FOLLOW THE INSTRUCTIONS BELOW.

ANYONE DISOBEYING ANY OF THE INSTRUCTIONS FOUND IN THE TEST INSTRUCTION BOOKLET MAY BE DISQUALIFIED AND RECEIVE A ZERO ON THE ENTIRE TEST.

FIRST SIGNAL: Follow the instructions of the test proctor.

SECOND SIGNAL: TURN TO NEXT PAGE, and begin work. This exam consists of 20 questions (1-20). Check to make sure that the test booklet goes up to and includes question number 20 and is not defective. You will have 40 minutes from this signal to complete all the questions.

THIRD SIGNAL: END OF THE TEST.

1. Yankee Stadium is located in the borough of

A. Brooklyn
B. Bronx
C. Manhattan
D. Queens

2. On Mondays through Fridays between January 19th and January 22nd, track maintenance is performed from 10 PM each evening to 5 AM the next morning. The B and D trains operate on tracks 2 and 3 that are effected by track maintenance. Both the B and D train are rerouted to the 8th Avenue line, while the F and M trains will continue to operate on tracks 1 and 4 at reduced speed during the maintenance.

Which of the following train routes are impacted by track maintenance at 4 AM?

A. B
B. B and D
C. F
D. F and M

Answer Question 3 based on the seven (7) train schedule table below.

Flushing Main St.	Mets Willets Pt.	111 St.	74 St. Broadway	61 St. Woodside	Queensboro Plaza	Times Square	34 St. Hudson Yards
12:12	12:14	12:16	12:21	12:25	12:32	12:41	12:47
12:26	12:28	12:30	12:35	12:39	12:46	12:55	1:01
12:40	12:43	12:44	12:50	12:53	1:00	1:09	1:16
1:00	1:03	1:04	1:10	1:13	1:20	1:29	1:36
1:20	1:23	1:24	1:30	1:33	1:40	1:49	1:56
1:40	1:43	1:44	1:50	1:53	2:00	2:09	2:16

3. Conductor James is performing platform duties at Times Square. A passenger asks him when the 7 train is due to arrive at Times Square station. The time is 1:15. What time does the next 7 train arrive?

A. 1:09
B. 1:15
C. 1:29
D. 1:36

4. What street is the Empire State Building located?

A. 14th Street
B. 23rd Street
C. 34th Street
D. 57th Street

Answer Question 5 based on the below diagrams.

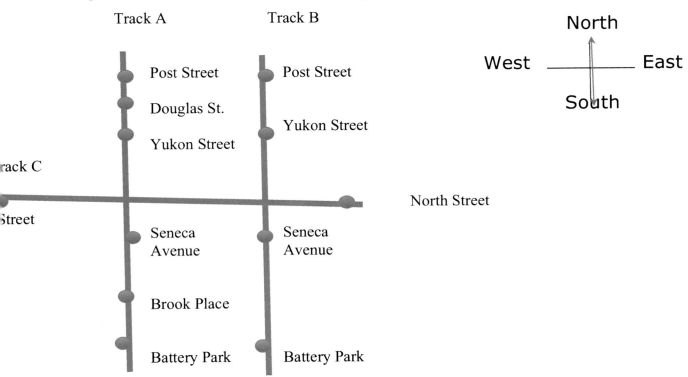

5. If a train is travelling north on Track B after leaving Seneca Avenue station, what is the next station?

A. Battery Park
B. Brook Place
C. Douglas Street
D. Yukon Street

6. What airport is located in the borough of Queens?

A. MacArthur Airport
B. Stewart International Airport
C. John F. Kennedy International Airport
D. Flushing Airport

Answer Questions 7-8 based on the TRAIN HORN OR WHISTLE SIGNALS below.

NOTE: Signals prescribed below are listed "Q" for short sounds and "T" for longer sounds.

SOUND INDICATION

Apply brakes immediately (STOP): T

Sounded when passing caution lights or flags to warn personnel of the approach of a train: TT

Road Car Inspector (subway mechanic) to respond to the train: QQQ

Signal Maintainer to respond to the train: TQ

Train Crew needs (Police) Assistance: TQTQ

7. A passenger informs the conductor of a medical emergency on the train. What train horn or whistle should be given?

A. TQ
B. TQTQ
C. TT
D. T

8. Conductor Phelps sounds the T horn when her train is leaving a station. What situation below would be appropriate for this horn signal?

A. Request for a route change.
B. A passenger is being dragged on the platform.
C. Train's air brakes unable to charge after repeated attempts.
D. A faulty train destination sign.

Answer Question 9 based on an incident report filed by a conductor.

Location: Coney Island Yard on Track 5; Car No. 68679
Observation: Inoperable train doors during a test.
Date and Time: November 6, 2018 at 1436 hours
Person Filing Report: Conductor Pass No. 43487
Outcome: Requested a Car Inspector (CI) to the train for assistance.

9. Which of the following best summarizes the incident report?

A. On November 6, 2018 at 1436 hours, Conductor pass number 43487 conducted a test of the train's doors. The doors were determined to be inoperable and a CI was requested for assistance.

B. On November 6, 2018 at 1346 hours, Conductor pass number 43487 conducted a test of the train's doors. The doors were determined to be inoperable and a CI was requested for assistance.

C. On November 6, 2018 at 1436 hours, Conductor pass number 43487 conducted a test of the train's doors. The doors were determined to be inoperable in Train Car No. 68679 and a CI was requested for assistance.

D. On November 6, 2018 at 1436 hours, Conductor pass number 43487 conducted a test of the train's doors. The doors were determined to be inoperable in Train Car No. 68679 on track 5 in the Coney Island Yard. A CI was requested for assistance.

Answer Question 10 based on a New York City Transit Bulletin issued to its train service employees.

NYCT Rapid Transit Operations (RTO) Bulletin for Suspicious Packages

All Train Service Employees **must** be alert for suspicious bags, packages or briefcases left anywhere in the Transit system. Employees who are given with a package from an unknown individual or who encounter a suspicious item left on the tracks, platforms or trains:

- Must immediately notify the Rail Control Center (RCC)
- Must not move, open, tamper or touch a package
- Must move away from a suspicious package and separate the area
- Must wait for and follow the instructions from the NYPD and/or RCC

The following steps must be followed if a suspicious package occurs on a train:

- Proceed the train to the nearest station if a train is between stations
- When the train is properly stopped in the station, the train crew will discharge passengers and the Conductor will make a manual Public Address announcement
- If possible, advise customers of alternative routes
- Follow the instructions from the NYPD and/or the RCC

10. A passenger informs a conductor of an unattended package on her train. Which of the following is the proper action to take?

    A. Notify the train operator immediately
    B. Notify the NYPD immediately
    C. Locate the package and check its contents for anything suspicious
    D. Follow the instructions from the NYPD and/or RCC

Answer Question 11 based on the DELAY ANNOUNCEMENTS PROCEDURE.

During train delays, delay announcements **must** be given. Delay announcements must include the reason for the delay. All train service employees must remember that when a delay to train service occurs, train crews **must** keep their customers informed and avoid play pre-recorded delay announcements on cars that are equipped with the automated announcement system. The Conductor is the individual who is charged with making train announcements. However, a Train Operator may have available information that the Conductor is not aware. In these circumstances, the Train Operator will make an announcement(s).

The first delay announcement will be made immediately. The train crew must identify themselves as the Train Operator or Conductor to the customer through the public address system, give the reason for a delay and give alternative routes. A manual announcement must be made within two (2) minutes of the first announcement and then at a minimum of every five (5) minutes if a delay is not resolved.

Public address systems may not work due to battery drain when power has been removed from the tracks and a delay has exceeded thirty (30) minutes. Train crews must confirm that their passengers are aware of the status of a delay by walking through the train and informing individuals in each car every ten (10) minutes.

11. Conductor Jenkins is informed of a stalled train that has delayed his train. An announcement is immediately made at 2:05 PM to the passengers to inform them of the delay. The Conductor then makes another announcement at 2:12 PM. The actions of the Conductor are

A. Correct, he immediately makes his second announcement within seven minutes of the first announcement.
B. Correct, he makes the minimum required two announcements when a delay occurred.
C. Incorrect, he did not make the required second announcement at 2:10 PM.
D. Incorrect, he did not make the required second announcement at 2:07 PM.

Answer Questions 12-13 based on the Bulletin on the UNIFORM POLICY for conductors.

During June 1st to September 30th, inclusive, conductors may remove their uniform coats. The regulation summer short-sleeved shirts must be worn with the regulation uniform trousers. Suspenders are not permitted if the uniform coat is removed. Shoes must be black, but sandals, suede, sneakers or canvas must not be worn. Conductors assigned to train service are not required to wear uniform caps during the above-mentioned period.

Conductors may work without a uniform tie if the uniform coat is removed. However, only the top collar button may be opened. The tie may not be removed if the uniform coat is worn.

Conductors assigned to platform duty must wear the uniform cap at all times. Conductors must furnish their badge numbers to anyone who requests it.

In addition, when the initial allotment or replacement uniform components are not readily available, employees must wear garments that are indistinguishable from the NYCT-issued uniform garments (examples of garments not permitted to be worn include but are not limited to cargo pants, carpenter pants, pants with cell phone or multi use pockets, tactical pants and paramedic/police pants).

12. Which of the following uniform components would be against the uniform policy outlined in the above bulletin?

A. Uniform tie worn with a uniform coat.
B. A platform conductor wearing his uniform cap on September 1st.
C. A train service conductor wearing brown shoes while on duty.
D. A conductor wearing NYCT issued summer short-sleeved shirts on June 1st without his uniform coat.

13. Conductors are not required to wear their uniform coats

A. during October 1st and May 31st.
B. if they are wearing suspenders.
C. only if a uniform cap is worn.
D. during the month of August.

Answer Questions 14-15 based on the below map.

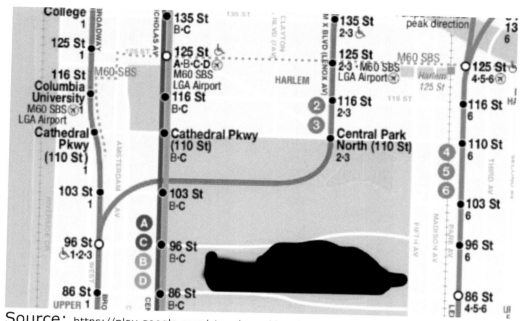

Source: https://play.google.com/store/apps/details?id=tech.beesknees.nycdynamicsubwaymap.free&hl=en_US

14. Passengers can transfer to the M60 SBS route from all of the subway stations below EXCEPT

A. 116 Street Columbia University Station on the 1 train line.
B. 116 Street Station on the 1 train line.
C. 125 Street Station on the A, B, C, D, 2, 3, 4, 5 and 6 train line.
D. 125 Street Station on the 1 train line.

15. A passenger takes the B train at 86 Street Station and she needs to continue her trip on the A train. Based on the map above, what station can she transfer to the A train?

A. 110 Street-Cathedral Parkway
B. 125 Street
C. 135 Street
D. Central Park North-110 Street

Answer Questions 16-17 based on the SERVICE DELIVERY ANNOUNCEMENT Bulletin.

Train Crews must adhere to the below procedure when making onboard public address announcements.

When making manual announcements, a train crew member must follow the below steps:

1. Depress the public address (PA) push button and observe the push button illuminate green.
2. Listen for an audible tone.
3. After the tone, wait two (2) seconds.
4. Press the Push to Talk push button and being to speak into the microphone.

ROUTINE ANNOUNCEMENTS

Approaching the station:

- This is _____. (name of station)
- Transfer/Connection is available to the _____ train(s).

When approaching a major transfer point, Conductors in addition to giving the above announcement, he/she will make the following announcement:

- Passengers if you are not exiting at (name of station) please move away from the doors and allow exiting customers to leave the train quickly. Thank you for your cooperation.

In the station with the door open:

- This is a (Borough/Terminal)-bound _____ (Local/Express) train.
- The next step is _____. (name of next station)
- Stand clear please.

WHEN SOMEONE HOLDS THE DOORS:

- Do not use the public address to speak directly to the passenger.
- Make the below announcement.
  Passengers, please do not hold the train doors open. Please release the doors so that the train can leave the station.

COURTESY ANNOUNCEMENTS

Courtesy announcements are only make when service is on or close to schedule and only once or twice per hour.

Passengers, the time is ____. Thank you for riding with MTA New York City Transit.

16. Conductor Nichols sees a passenger holding the train doors. He depresses the PA push button, observes the push button illuminate green, listens for the audible tone. And after waiting for two seconds, he presses the push to talk push button and speaks directly into the microphone. He informs the passenger, "To the passenger in the second car, please do not hold the train doors open. Please release the doors so that the train can leave the station."

The actions of the conductor are

A. Correct, he addressed directly to the passenger holding the train doors in a courteous manner.
B. Correct, he followed the proper procedures when making an onboard public address announcement and the correct announcement when someone holds the train doors.
C. Incorrect, he addressed the passenger directly instead of addressing the announcement to passengers.
D. Incorrect, he did not state, "Stand clear please."

17. Courtesy announcements are made to passengers when

A. trains are running behind schedule to calm passengers.
B. trains are running on or close to schedule.
C. they are made at least three times per hour.
D. a train is delayed in between stations.

Answer Questions 18-19 based on the DOOR OPERATION LEAVING TERMINALS procedure.

The departing Conductor from a terminal station will enter the operating cab two minutes before the scheduled departure time. He/she will perform the following procedures:

1. Acknowledge the Conductors' Indication Board on the correct platform side.
2. Insert the Master Door Control (MDC) key and rotate the MDC key switch from "Term" to the "On" position by using the MDC on the correct platform side.
3. Then open the train's side doors.
4. One minute before the scheduled departure time, the Conductor makes all pre-departure public address announcements.

- All Train Crews must be on their trains and/or their respective operating positions two minutes before their scheduled departure time.

18. Conductor Daniels enters her operating cab two minutes before the scheduled departure time. She acknowledges the Conductors' Indication Board by pointing at the board with her extended index finger. What is the next step that she must perform?

A. Insert the MDC key and rotate the key switch from "Term" to "On."
B. Check the train's destination signs for accuracy.
C. Make a pre-departure public address announcement.
D. Test the intercom and request the Train Operator to acknowledge receipt.

19. What time must a Conductor be on his/her train if the departure time of a Manhattan bound F train is 1500 hours?

A. 1455 hours
B. 1458 hours
C. 1459 hours
D. 1500 hours

Answer Question 20 based on the number 4 train schedule.

Utica Avenue	Franklin Avenue	Atlantic Avenue-Barclays Center	Bowling Green	Brooklyn Bridge	Grand Central-42 Street
6:42	6:46	6:51	6:59	7:03	7:12
6:52	6:56	7:01	7:09	7:14	7:23
7:02	7:05	7:11	7:19	7:24	7:34
7:05	7:08	7:14	7:22	7:27	7:37
7:12	7:15	7:21	7:29	7:34	7:44
7:14	7:17	7:23	7:31	7:36	7:46
7:20	7:23	7:29	7:38	7:43	7:52
7:23	7:26	7:32	7:41	7:46	7:55

Notes:

Layover: A short period of time between the end of one trip and the next scheduled trip.

Headway: A time interval between two subway trains of the same subway line in the train schedule.

20. What is the headway at Brooklyn Bridge station between the number 4 trains leaving Utica Avenue at 7:14 and 7:20?

A. 2 minutes
B. 3 minutes
C. 6 minutes
D. 7 minutes

STOP! END OF TEST

ANSWER KEY

1. B
2. B
3. C
4. C
5. D
6. C
7. B
8. B
9. D
10. D
11. D
12. C
13. D
14. D
15. B
16. C
17. B
18. A
19. B
20. D

EXPLANATIONS

1. Yankee Stadium is located in the borough of Bronx. The 2016 Conductor exam did not contain questions on New York City points of interest. However, I recommend that you study major points of interest in New York City in the event that New York City Transit decides to include these types of questions for future exams. Before the 2016 Conductor exam, past exams included points of interest questions.

The correct answer is **B**.

2. The information provided in the question states that both the B and D trains are impacted by track maintenance. While the F and M trains will continue to run on its tracks. The correct answer is **B**.

3. The question asks about the next arriving 7 train at Times Square. Focus on the Times Square column in the train schedule and ignore the rest of the other columns that are not relevant to answering the question.

If the time is 1:15, the next 7 train to arrive at Times Square station is at 1:29. The correct answer is **C**.

4. The Empire State building is located on 34th Street in midtown Manhattan. The correct answer is **C**.

5. Expect to see a map on the Conductor exam. Your job is to focus on a specific part of the map that helps you answer the question. The question is about Track B, so you can ignore Track A. A train travelling north after Seneca Avenue would arrive at Yukon Street.

If you chose Battery Park, you might have either misread the question or missed seeing the compass that gives you the direction in the map.

The correct answer is **D**.

6. Two airports are located in Queens; LaGuardia Airport and John F. Kennedy International Airport. For history buffs, Queens used to have a Flushing Airport in College Point near Flushing, but it was closed in 1984. The correct answer is **C**.

7. A Conductor would summon the police in a medical emergency. Looking at the information given, the appropriate train horn/whistle is TQTQ. The correct answer is **B**.

8. Upon a Conductor seeing the dragging of a passenger, he/she would sound the T horn for a Train Operator to apply the brakes immediately and stop the train. The correct answer is **B**.

INCORRECT ANSWERS:

A. The immediate application of brakes would not be appropriate to request a route change. This action is unsafe.

C. The inability to charge the train's air brakes would require a subway mechanic to assist. The appropriate train horn or whistle is QQQ.

D. A faulty train destination sign would involve a subway mechanic as an appropriate individual to troubleshoot. The appropriate train horn or whistle is QQQ.

9. This type of question asks you to best summarize a number of facts or observations provided. This question type may appear on the Conductor exam. It's important to acclimate yourself to answer these questions correctly.

The sequence of events that occur is a key important strategy to answer this question correctly. The questions asks for the best summary for an incident report.

Answer B is incorrect as the time of 1346 hours is incorrect, so this answer choice should be eliminated immediately.

The sequence of events are that a conductor was testing the train's doors and determined that it was not operable. The outcome was to request a car inspector for assistance. Now let's look at the remaining answer choices A, C and D.

Choice A is incorrect, as the summary fails to state where the train doors are inoperable. It is in car number 68679.

Choice C does not state what track the train is located on that has inoperable train doors.

The correct answer is **D**. The summary gives the complete information of the date and time, the employee's pass number who conducted the test, the car number that has defective doors, the track number and name of the yard and a request for a car inspector.

10. Among all of the answer choices, following the instructions of the NYPD or RCC is directed to employees in the bulletin. The correct answer is **D**.

INCORRECT ANSWERS:

A. The bulletin does not state that a Conductor is to notify the train operator of an unattended package. In fact, a Conductor must immediately notify the Rail Control Center, as stated in the first bullet point of the bulletin for suspicious packages.

B. The Bulletin does not direct Conductors to notify the NYPD.

C. Checking the package's contents is against policy. The Bulletin directs train crews to move away from a suspicious package and separate passengers from the area that the package is located.

11. The Conductor appropriately makes an announcement immediately after learning of a delay. However, the procedure is for the Conductor to make another announcement two minutes after the first announcement is made. Mr. Jenkins notifies passengers at 2:12 PM, which is seven minutes after the first announcement. His action is incorrect, so answer choices A and B can be eliminated immediately.

Answer C is a trap answer if you misread the information provided. Making an announcement at 2:10 PM would be five minutes after the first announcement is made. The rule is two minutes after the first announcement, and followed by a minimum of five minutes if a delay is not resolved.

The correct answer is **D**. At 2:07 PM, the second announcement should have been made to passengers.

12. Most Conductor exams in the past have included a question about Conductor uniforms. The uniform policy states that Conductors can only wear black shoes. Wearing brown shoes is a violation of the uniform policy. The correct answer is **C**.

INCORRECT ANSWERS:

A. When a uniform coat is worn, a uniform tie must be worn. This is in compliance with the uniform policy.

B. Platform conductors are required to wear their cap at all times.

D. Conductors are allowed to wear a summer short-sleeved shirt between June and September.

13. The first sentence in the Policy helps you answer this question. August is a month between June and September, so Conductors can remove their coat. The correct answer is **D**.

INCORRECT ANSWERS:

A. Between October and May, Conductors are required to wear their uniform coat.

B. The policy states only suspenders can be worn if Conductors are wearing their coat.

C. Nothing in the policy states that a uniform coat is not required if a uniform cap is worn.

14. Subway maps are likely to appear on your Conductor exam. Read the question first before scanning the map for the answer.

The question is about the M60 SBS route. Looking at the map, the M60 SBS stops along Cathedral Parkway-110 Street, 116 Street and all of the 125 Street stations except on the 1 train. The correct answer is **D**.

15. The next available opportunity to transfer to the A train after 86 Street station is the 125 Street station when looking at the map provided. The correct answer is **B**.

16. The test makers like to include long reading passages or long policies on the test. Most of the time, you do not need to read the entire information given to answer the test questions. Read the question first before scanning the information for the answer.

The policy that this question is concerning is a passenger holding the train doors. Read the **When Someone Holds the Doors** section of the bulletin. The first bullet point states that Conductors are not to address directly to a passenger. The Conductor stated, "To the passenger in the second car …" This is against policy, and the correct answer is **C**.

17. The last section of the Bulletin on Courtesy Announcements helps you answer this question. The policy is these types of announcement are made when train service is on or close to schedule. Therefore, the correct answer is **B**.

INCORRECT ANSWERS:

A. The policy prohibits courtesy announcements when trains are not running close to schedule.

C. Courtesy announcements are made only once or twice each hour. Three times is against the policy.

D. Nowhere does the Bulletin state that courtesy announcements can be made when a train is delayed.

18. This is a procedural question to see if you can follow procedures in order. The important point of this question is the Conductor has acknowledged the Conductors' Indication Board. What is the next step? The second step is to insert the key into the Master Door Control and to rotate the key to the "On" position. The correct answer is **A**.

INCORRECT ANSWERS:

B. Checking the destination signs is not included in the Bulletin as one of the steps. While one might argue that this is a responsibility of the train crew, the job of the test taker is to follow what is given in the information.

C. A pre-departure announcement is the last step in the procedure to follow before departure.

D. Testing the intercom is not a step outlined in the pre-departure procedure. This answer is incorrect.

19. The first sentence and last bullet point in the Bulletin answers this question. Train crews are to be on their trains two minutes before a departure time. If the departure time is 1500 hours for a F train, then the Conductor needs to be on board at least 1458 hours, or 1500-2=1458. The correct answer is **B**.

20. The definition of headway assists us in answering this question. As I stated in this book, NYCT does not expect test takers to have previous knowledge of the subway system. The question is asking you what how many minutes between two number 4 trains will arrive at Brooklyn Bridge station. We are concerned with two subway 4 trains departing at 7:14 and 7:20 from Utica Avenue station. Ignore the rest of the schedule since it does not help us answer the question.

The 7:14 Utica Avenue arrives at Brooklyn Bridge at 7:36, while the 7:20 train arrives at Brooklyn Bridge at 7:43. Therefore, calculate the difference:

$$7:43-7:36=7 \text{ minutes}$$

Answer choice C is a trap answer for those who misread the question. You might have subtracted the difference between the 7:20 and 7:14 trains that departed from Utica Avenue. This would be a six minute difference. However, the question is asking about the headway between both trains at **Brooklyn Bridge** station.

The correct answer is **D**.

ABOUT THE AUTHOR

Mr. Young started his civil service career after graduating from college. He has taken numerous City of New York and State of New York civil service exams over the past fifteen years, including Train Operator and Conductor. Mr. Young successfully went through the hiring process for a number of civil service positions.

His commitment to candidates using this book is to develop high quality test preparation materials with a focus on the content and skills that are frequently tested on the exams. And he is confident that his book, **Surfing Through New York Transit Exams**, will prepare applicants to successfully score high on their exam for a career with the Metropolitan Transportation Authority.

Mr. Young earned a Bachelor of Science degree with academic distinction from Binghamton University, State University of New York. He holds a Master of Public Administration degree from New York University.

ABOUT THE BOOK

Competition for Train Operator and Conductor jobs with New York City Transit is stiff. The number of individuals applying for employment significantly exceeds the number of vacancies available. The first step of the hiring process for Train Operator and Conductor is to take and to score extremely high on a civil service exam.

This test preparation book prepares you to earn a high score on your exam whether you are taking an open competitive exam or are a Transit employee preparing for your next promotion. The book is a valuable resource for individuals applying for civil service careers with the New York City government. Future and provisional City employees will learn how to navigate the complex and long process to secure permanent civil service status. A civil service career offers job security, comprehensive benefits and a valuable defined benefit pension for qualified employees.

- Understand and navigate the New York City civil service process to obtain a stable and long-term career

- Learn about the job responsibilities for train operator and conductor and how to qualify for the civil service exams

- Guide you through the hiring and appointment processes for train operator and conductor

- Practice on Train Operator and Conductor exams that closely reflect the difficulty level and content of the real exams

- Review detailed explanations to each test question